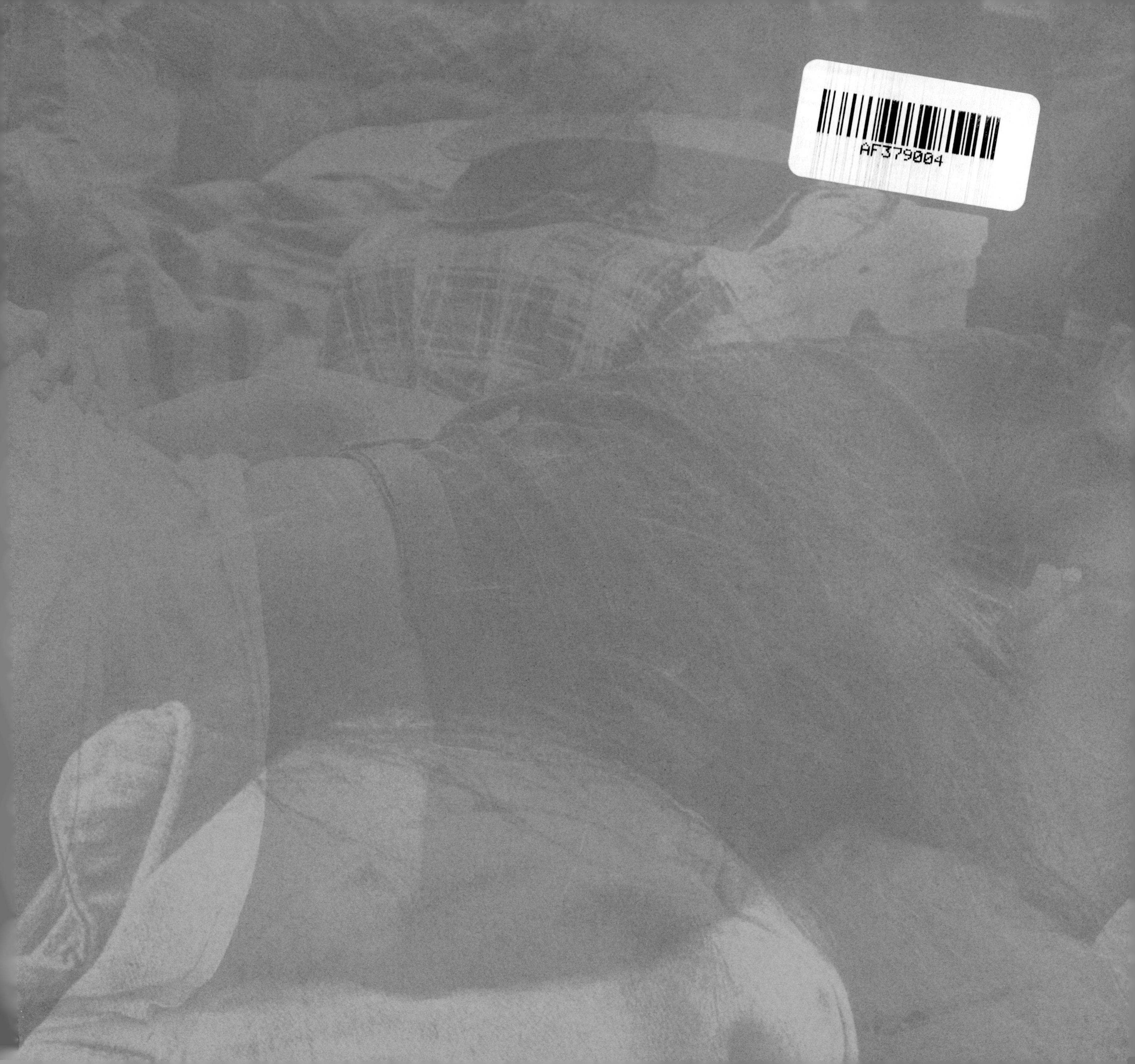

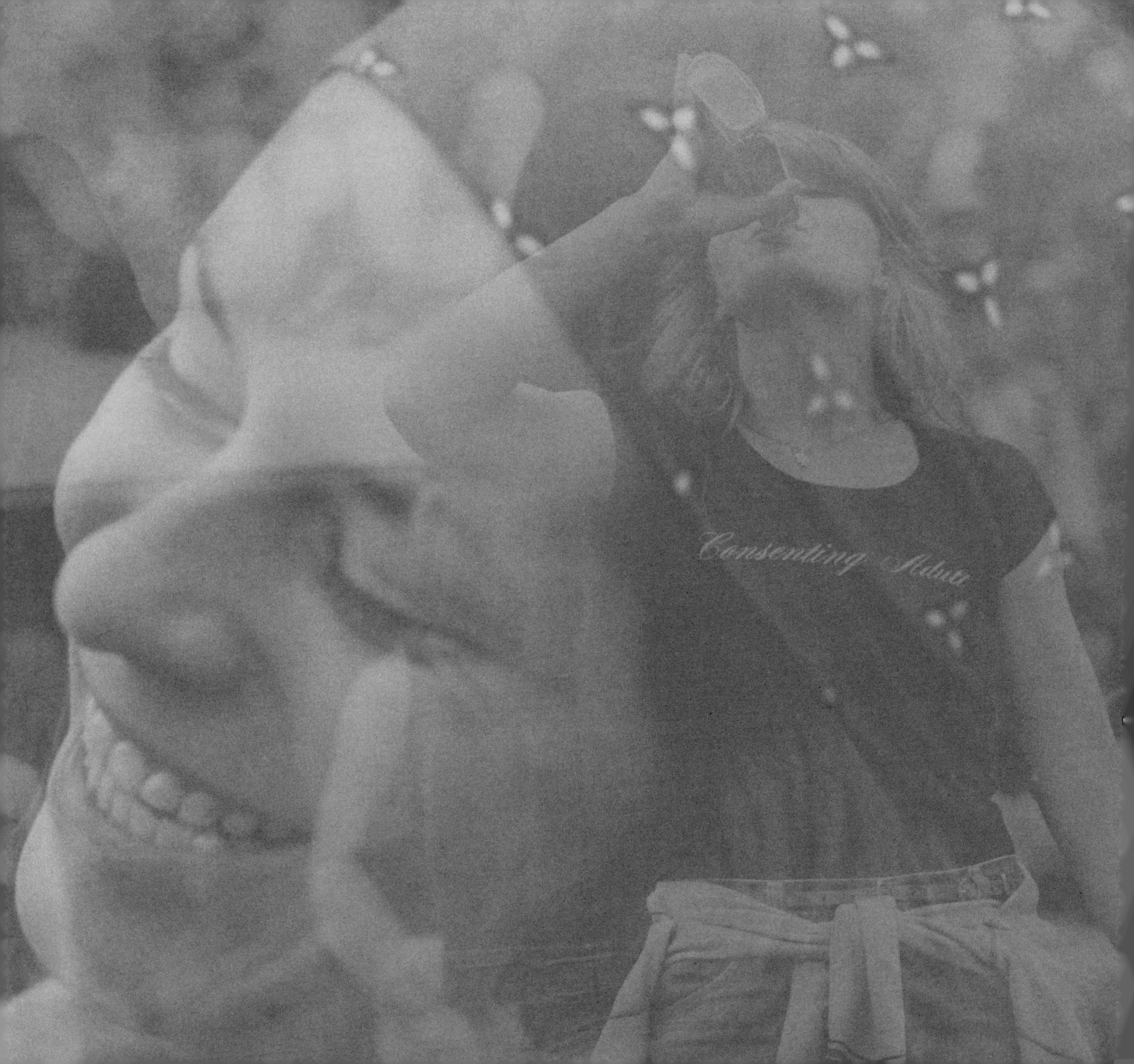
Consenting Adults

ROLLING STONES FANS

JOSEPH SZABO

THIS BOOK IS DEDICATED TO ALL THE ROLLING STONES FANS IN THIS BOOK

There is nothing intrusive about Joe Szabo. His eye is sharp, but his voice is soft – he can fit right into a crowd and find a host of images that are both compelling and inspirational. I was first introduced to his work through his 2003 book "Teenage" and was immediately struck by how unselfconsciously elegant his subjects were. Though sometimes defiant, they have a confidence and a cool aloofness about them. It is a kind of freedom I long to evoke in my fashion stories for Vogue.

The moments captured in pictures of Rolling Stones fans are a reminder of life before cell phones and "Selfies" and "It Bags" and all the paraphernalia of concerts today, that are so over-produced – more about the special effects and the stage design than the music itself, devoid of the pure joy and raw emotion you see in Joe's pictures. Just as his last book is on the shelf of every young fashion editor so, I'm sure, will this one be.

– Grace Coddington –

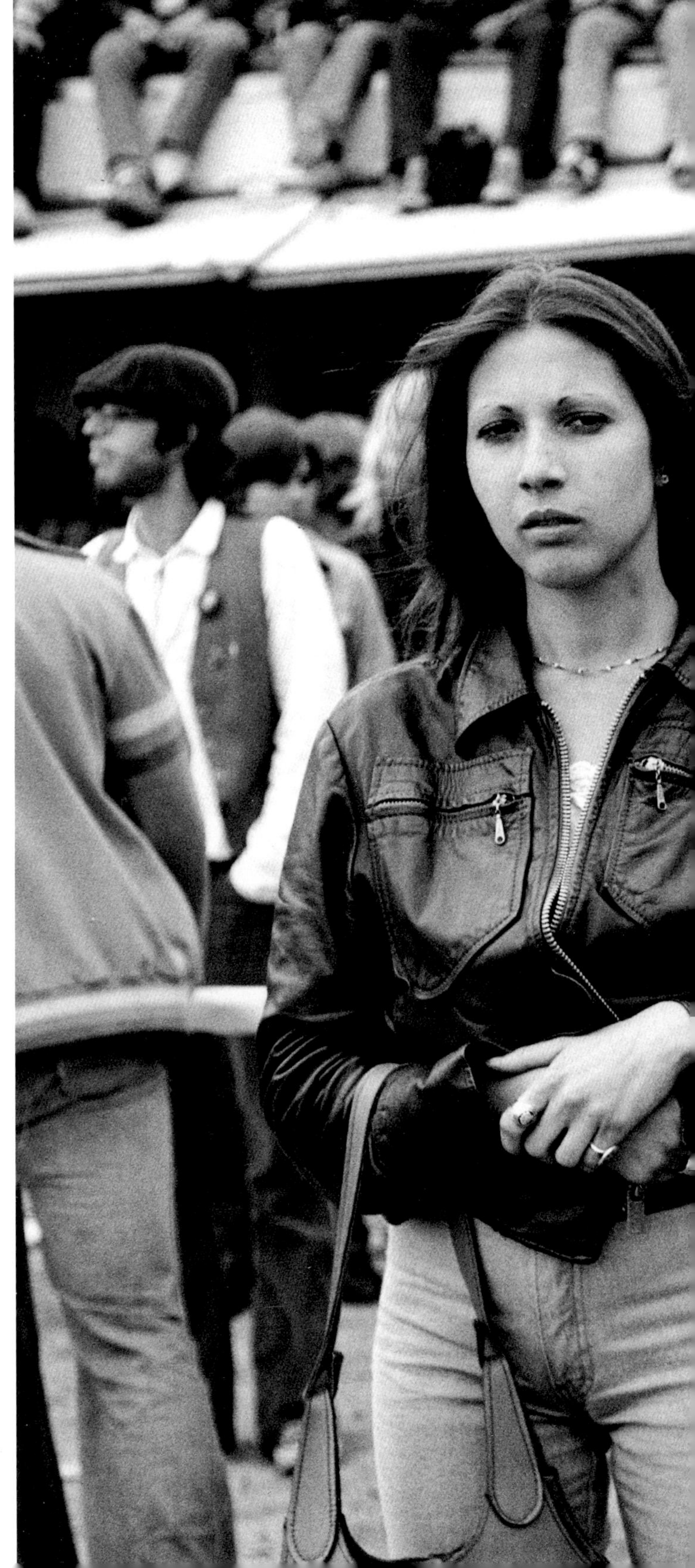

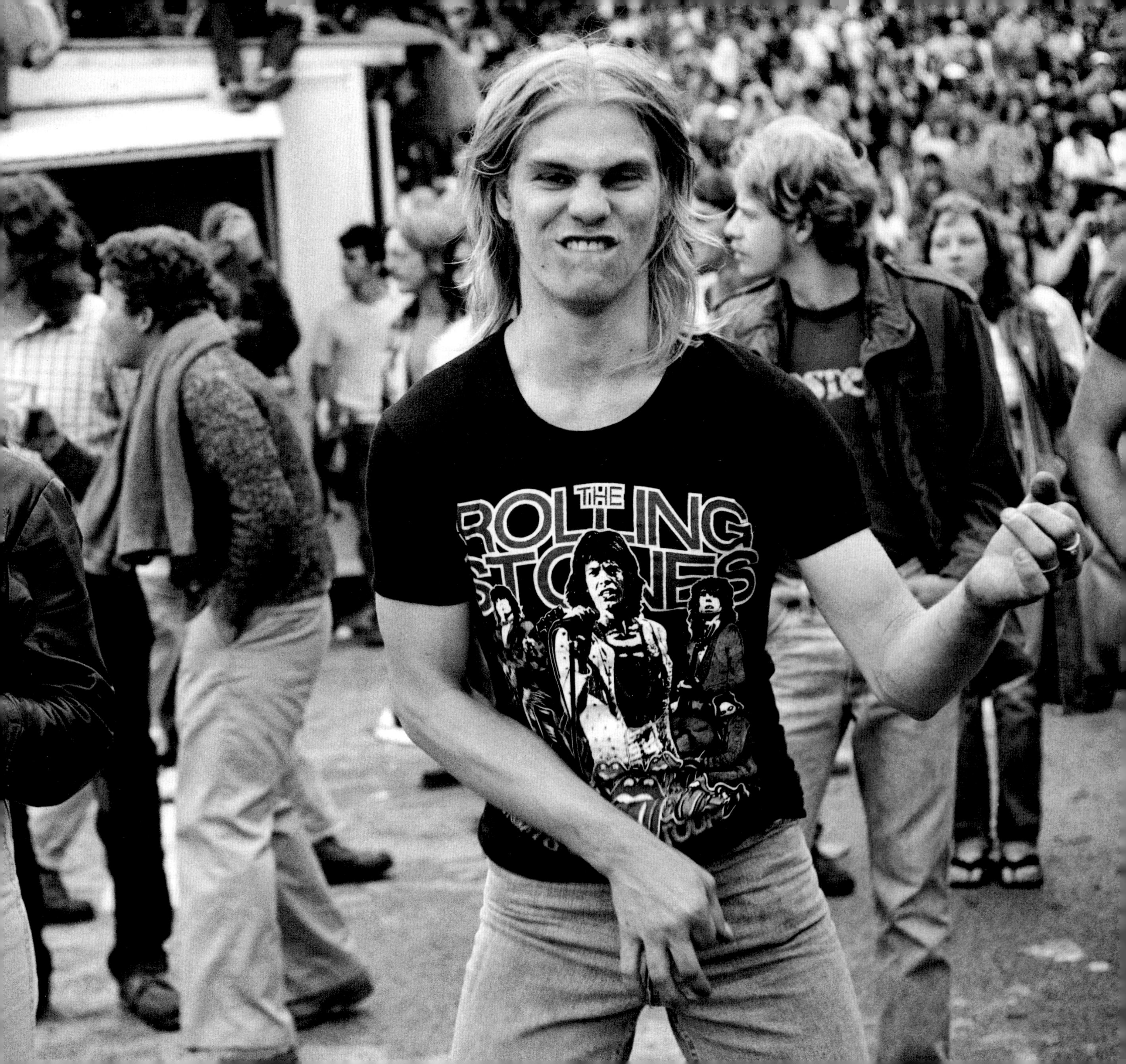

JOSEPH SZABO ON PHOTOGRAPHING "ROLLING STONES FANS"

In 1978 as the school year drew to a close, Bill Carraro and Chris Davies, two of my photography students, who also worked as editors for the yearbook, asked, "Mr. Szabo would you like to go to a Rolling Stones concert? We have an extra ticket." Being a lover of rock and roll, I was intrigued. But before I could even ask why, they said, "The only thing is, the concert is in Philadelphia and we need a ride to get to there." Bill and Chris were both seniors and I knew their request was not just about driving them, but that we would share the experience as friends. After discussing it with my wife Nancy, who thought it was a good idea and promising photo opportunity, I enthusiastically said, "Yes!"

When we got to JFK stadium on June 17th everything was wet and soggy from the overnight rain. The place was packed—news reports estimated the crowd at over 90,000. There were no assigned seats—if you didn't have a seat saved by your friends, you didn't have a seat. The closer we got to the stage where The Stones were playing, the denser the crowds. It felt like being in Times Square on New Year's where you are bombarded by all these sights and sounds. You don't know which way to look. That's how it was; all these fans, all these people surrounding me.

Awed, I took out my camera and started photographing. I had been capturing the lives of my highschool students in Malverne, New York since 1972 and the concert just followed that idea of seeing their lives beyond the school's walls.

I've always felt that music is a mysterious thing, in the way the sounds are put together, in what it can express. When you add the right words, it's inspirational, it's infectious. There is no doubt that The Stones influenced my photography that day. But Mick Jagger and company were not the reason why I was there. The show was down on the field, among the people. You see these faces and you connect with them, you feel a certain sympathy or empathy for them.

When a photograph captures the energy of its subject, it's not because of the subject's energy alone. It's because my energy and their energy came together at the same time to capture the moment. I had to be in that moment, too. I couldn't be objective and separated. I had to be part of the whole experience, the music and the mood.

I was very close, physically close to all the people I photographed. They trusted me. But there were some situations where I would get a hostile look from somebody. And momentarily I questioned myself, "Do I take this person's photograph or not?" But I thought, "This is why I am here," to mirror this whole situation. I want people who didn't come to this concert or people who did come, to say, "That's the way it was. That's a true picture."

From my perspective going to the concert was a gift. The chaotic unpredictability of it was part of its charm. Recently, I was inspired to revisit the contact sheets from that day and choose images that spoke to me after so many years. For me, the honesty of the pictures still rings true.

This is what teenagers were like on this day, in this place, in this time. Substitute today's clothes and hairstyles, and I think you'll find teenagers doing pretty much the same things.

I am still in touch with Bill and Chris, and we remain good friends to this day. I am forever grateful to them for our trip, as well as, to all the Rolling Stone fans who were so open to my camera.

– Joseph Szabo –

Edited from outtakes of the documentary The Joseph Szabo Project. *As told to George Pozderec.*

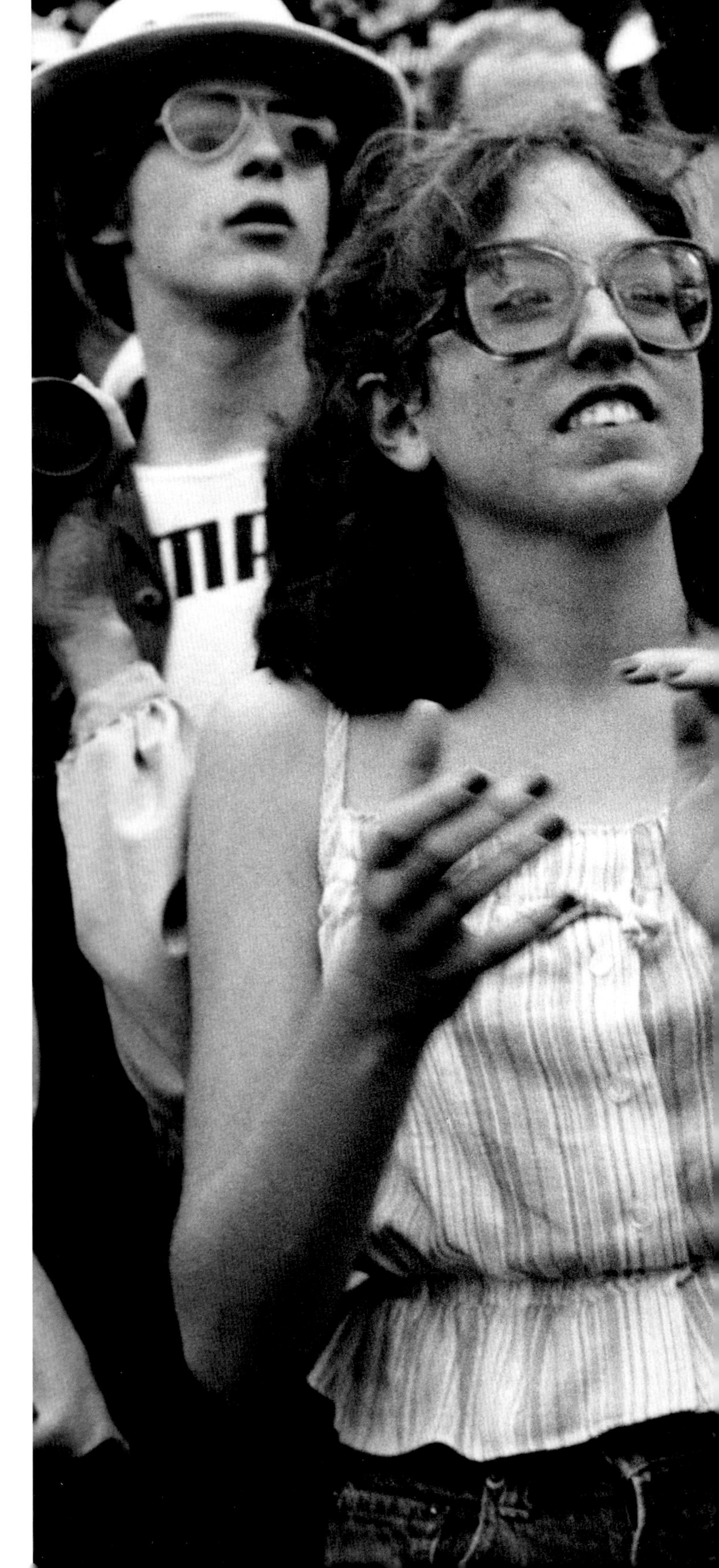

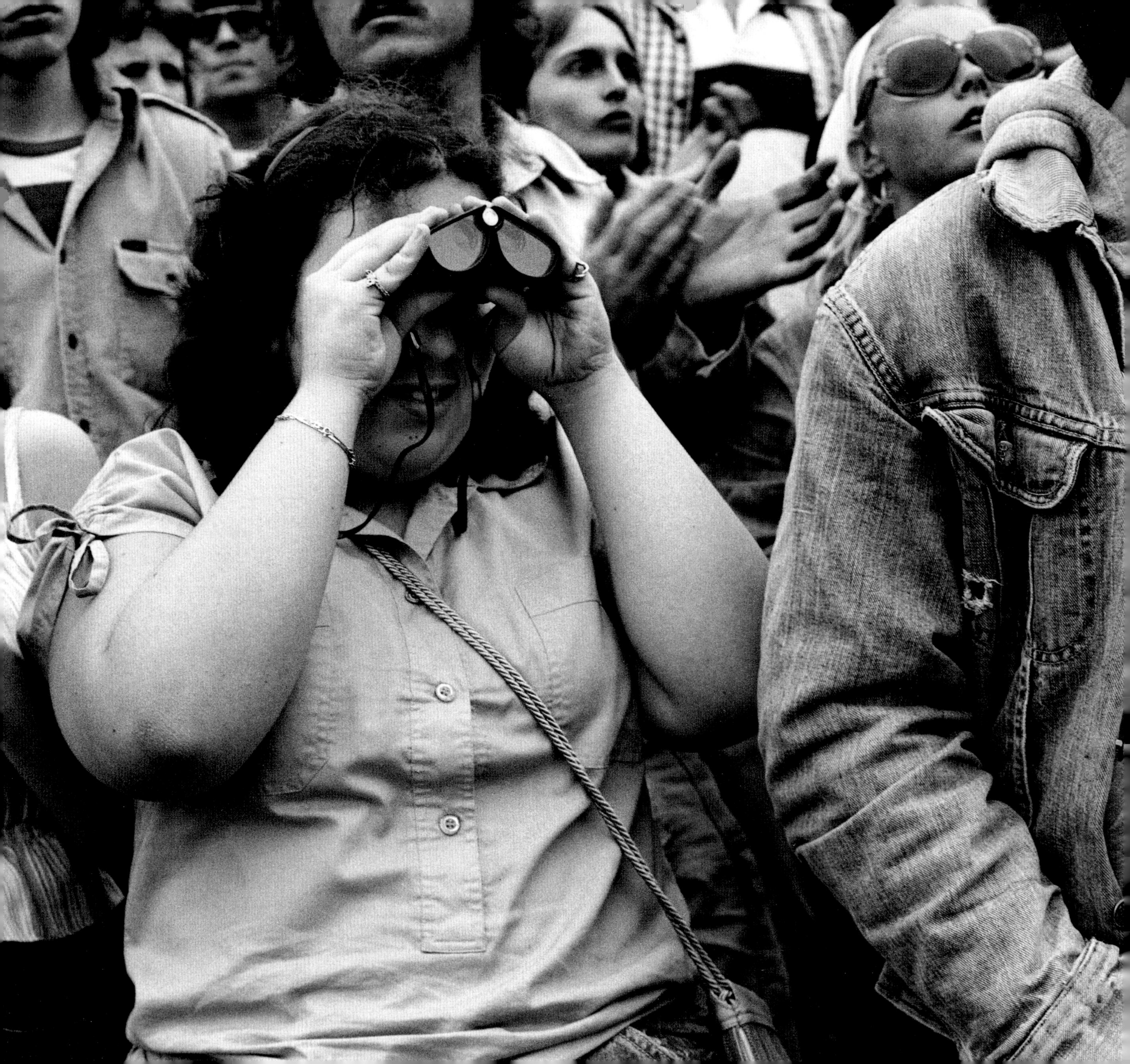

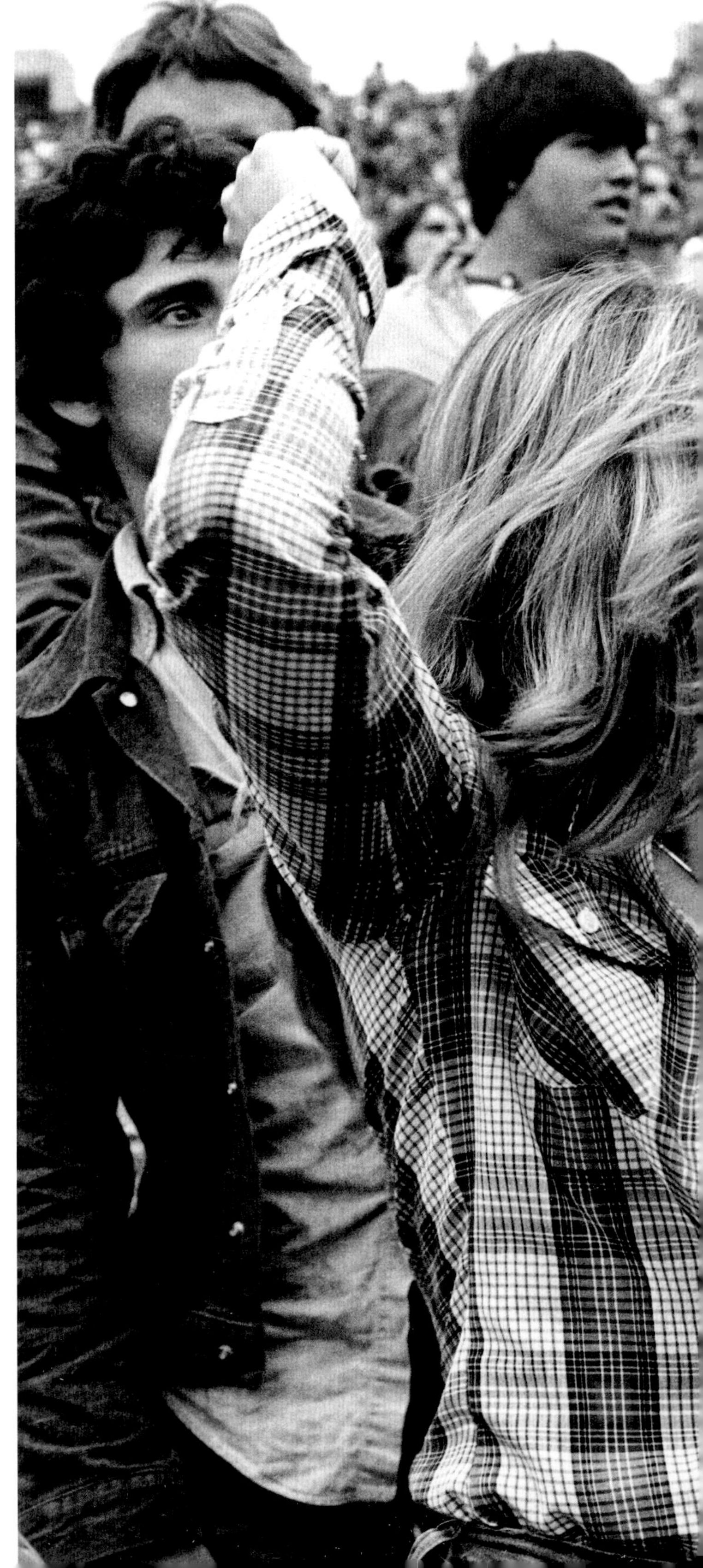

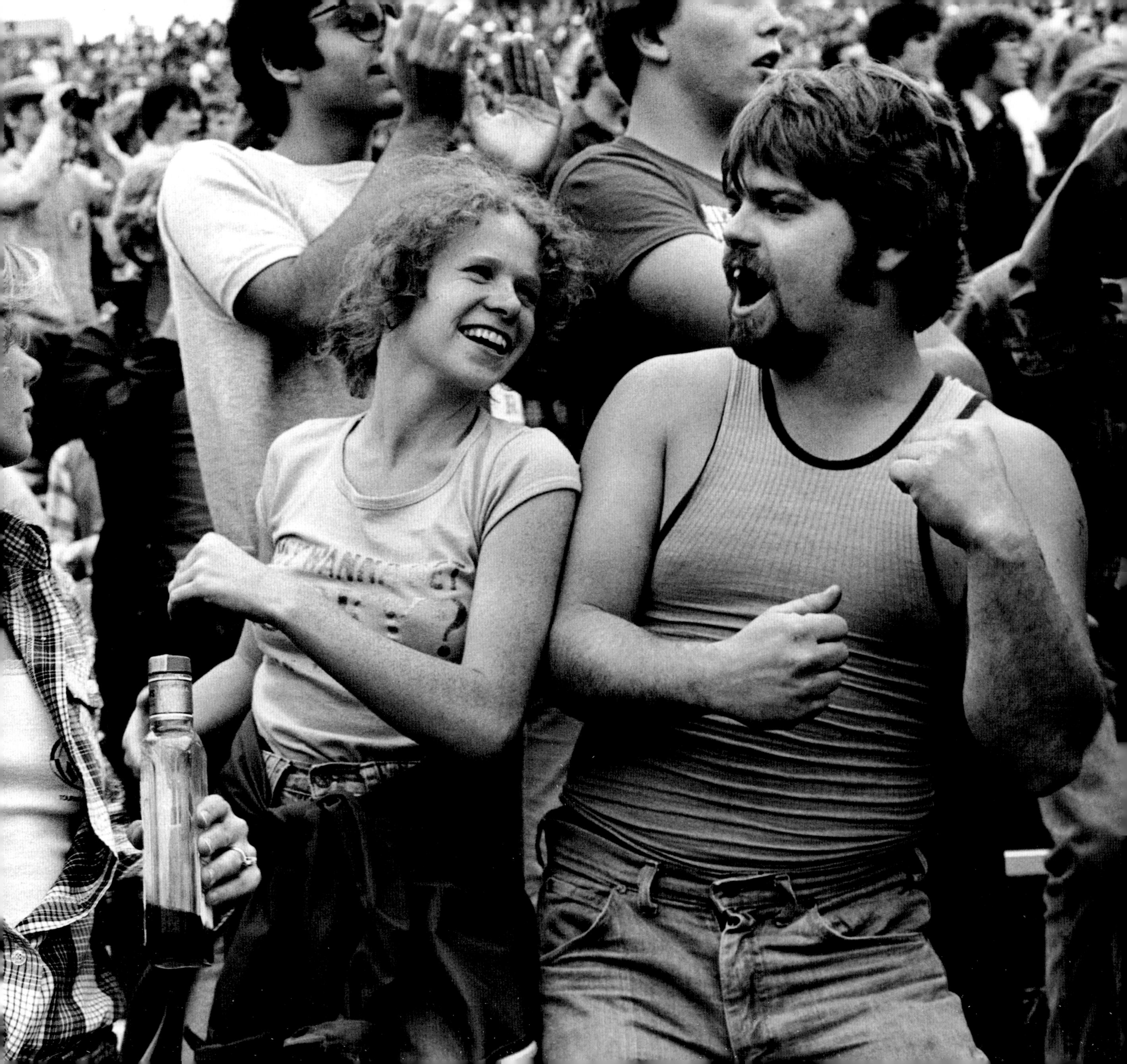

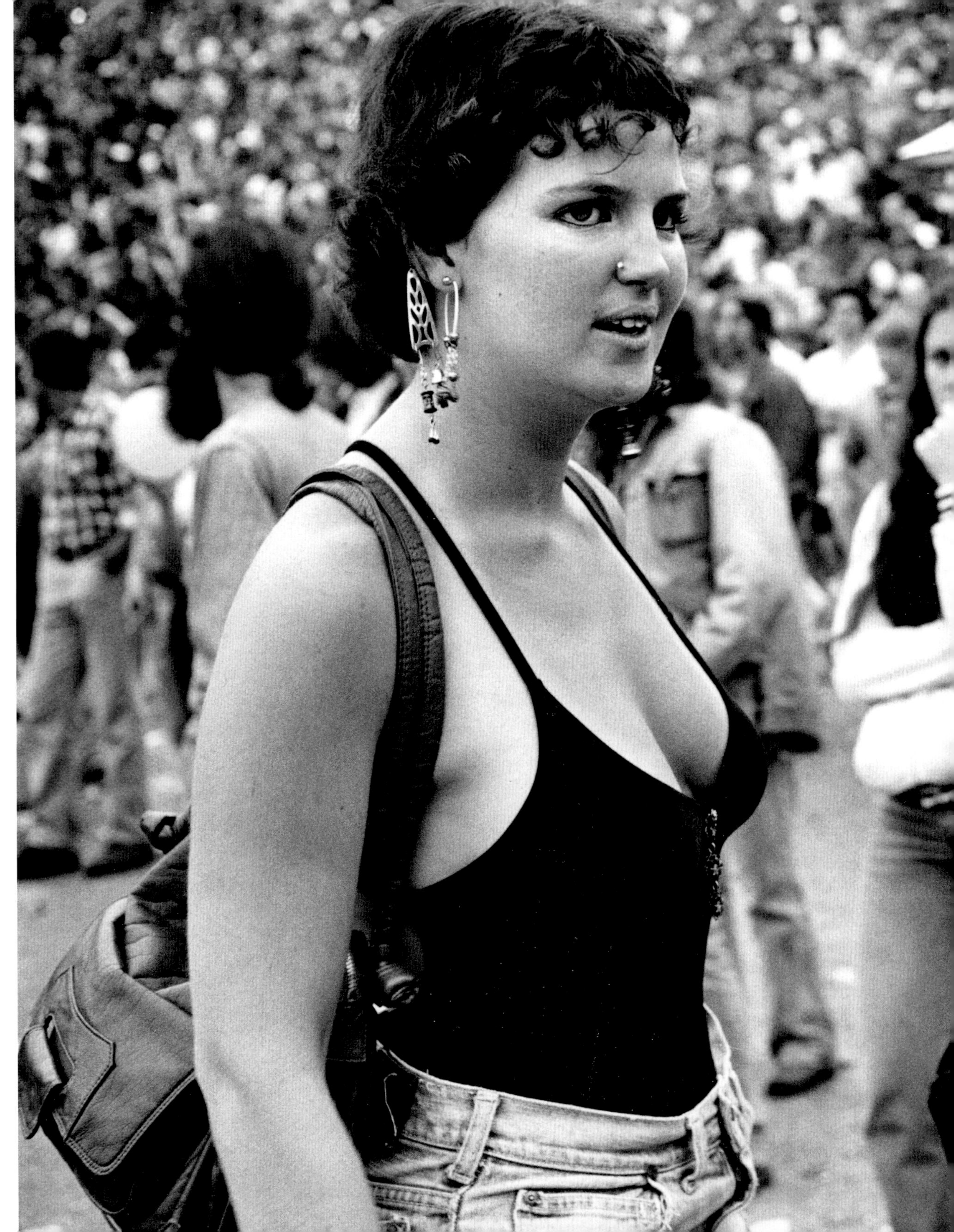

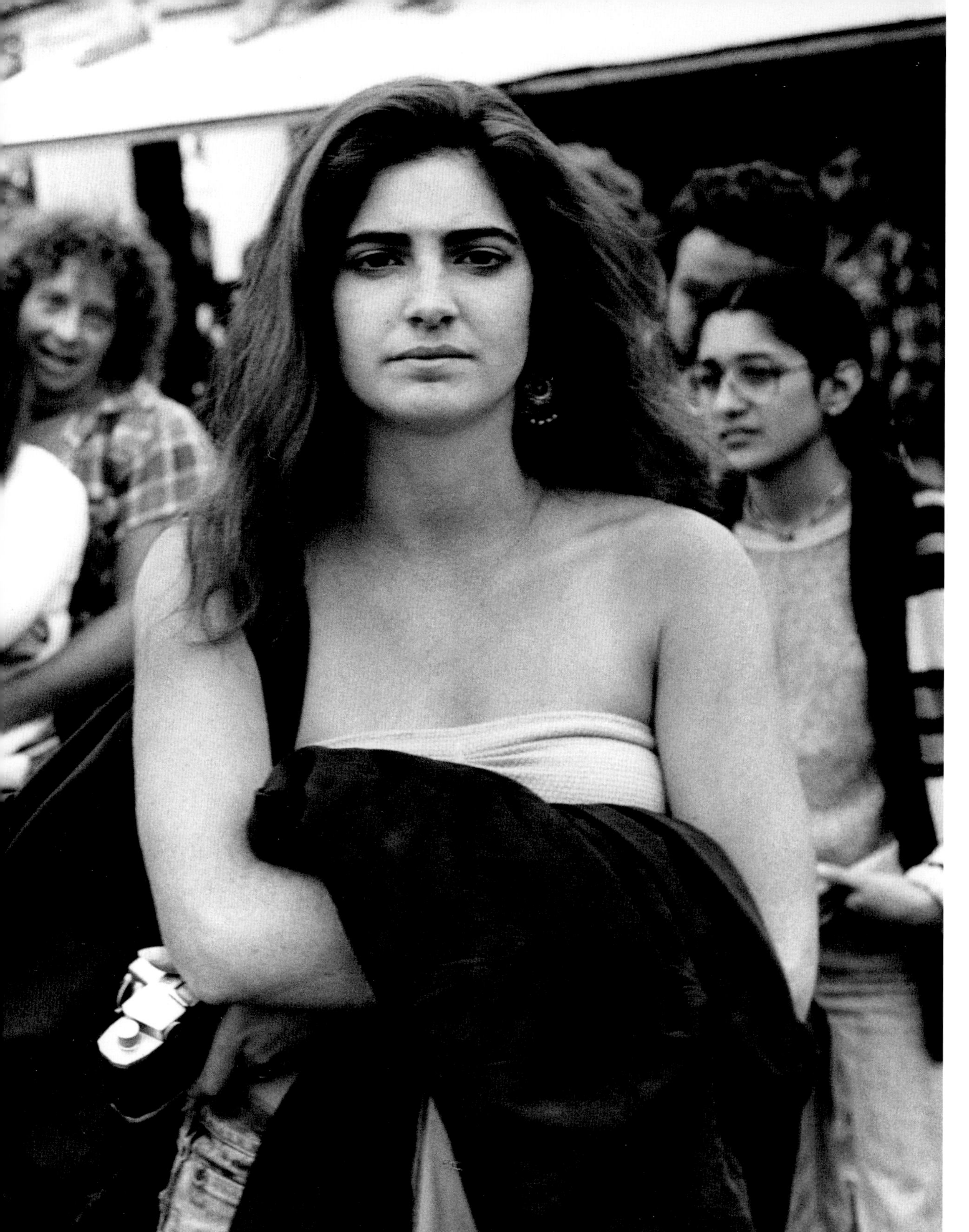

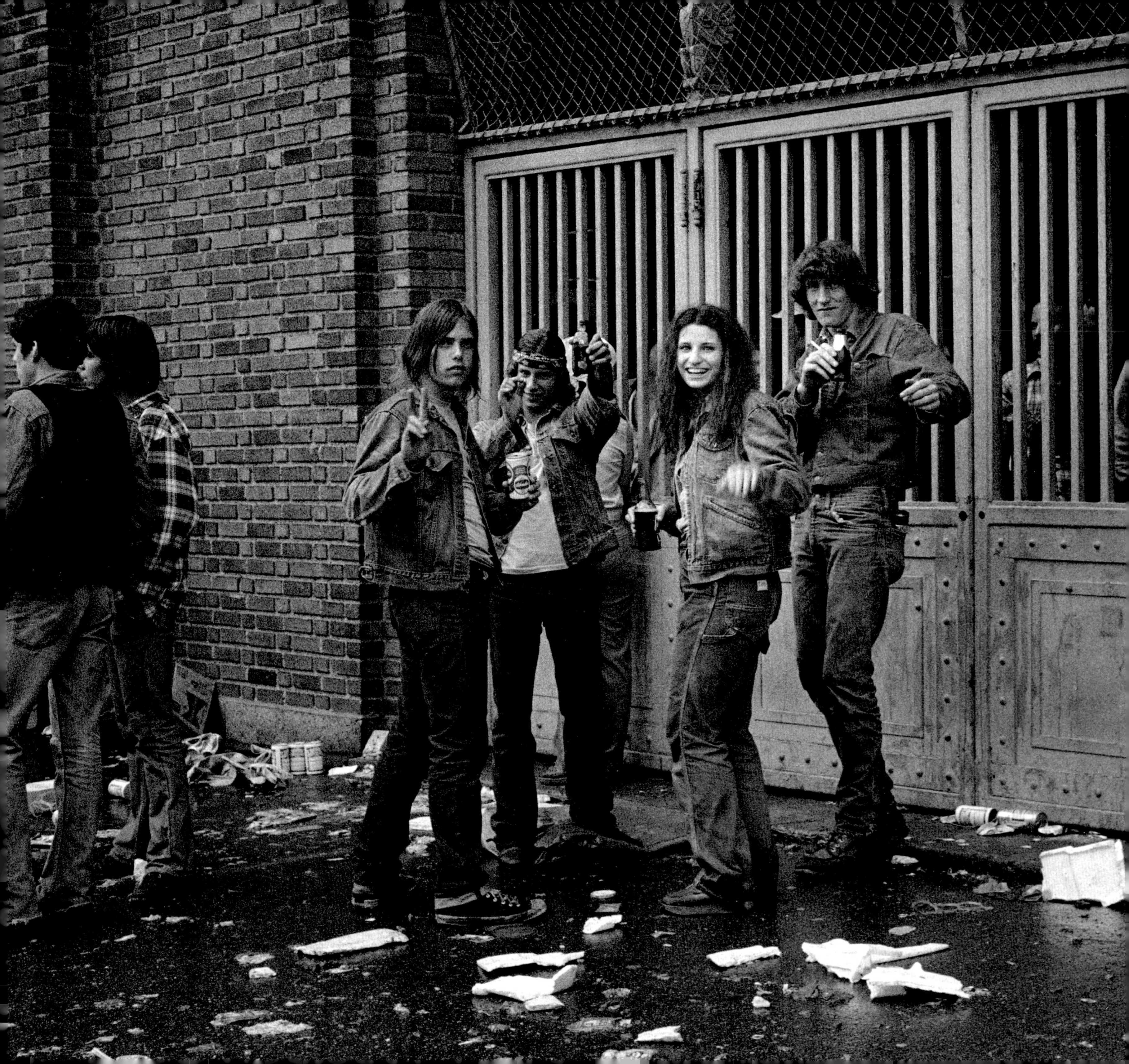

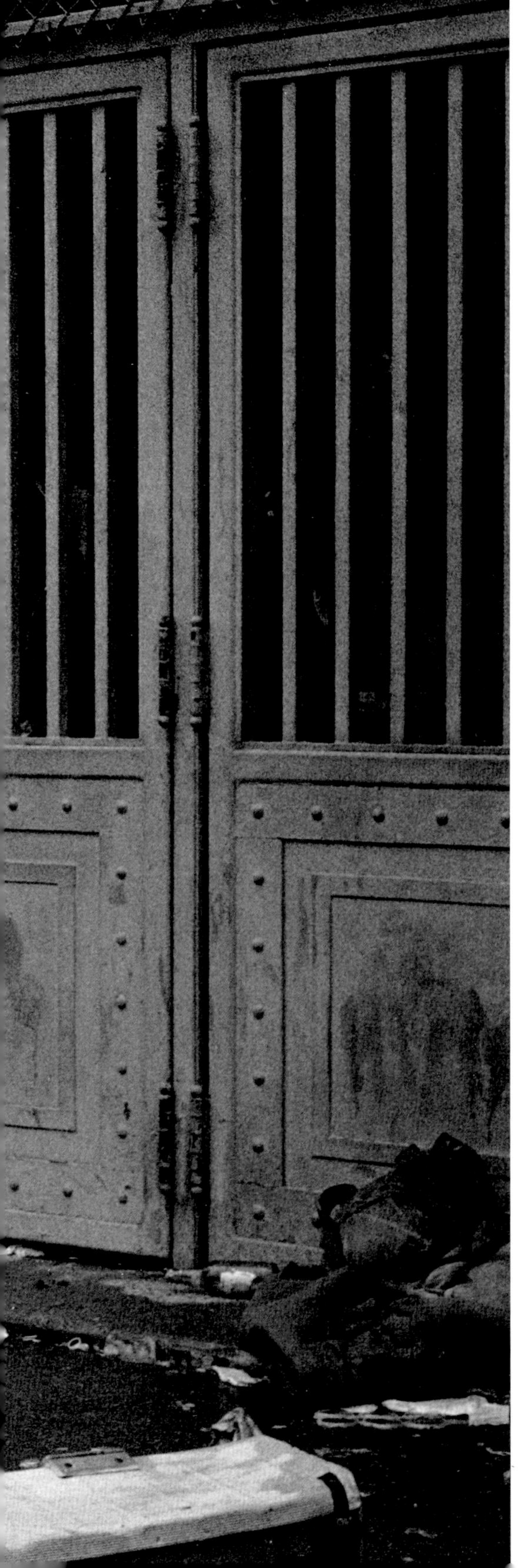

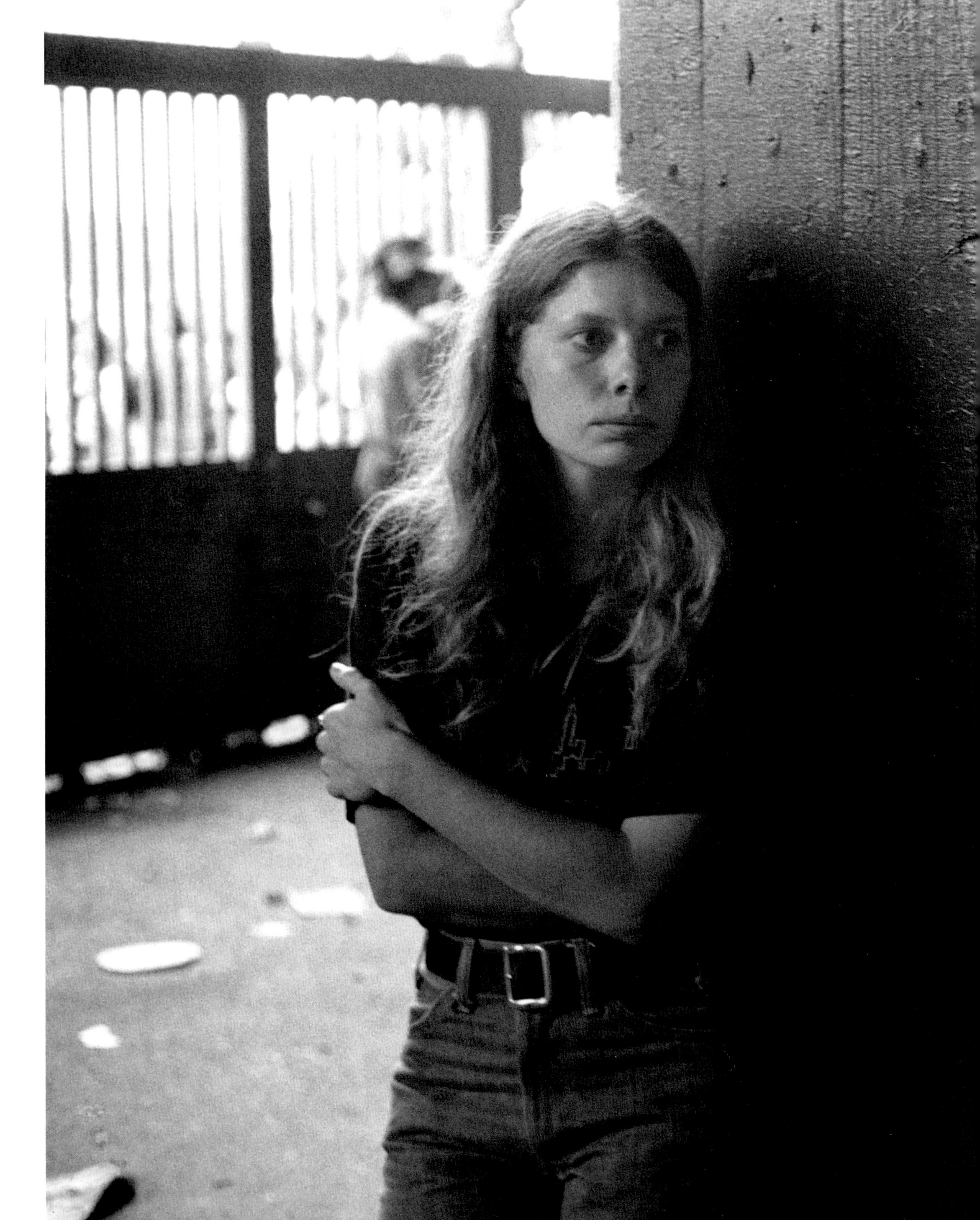

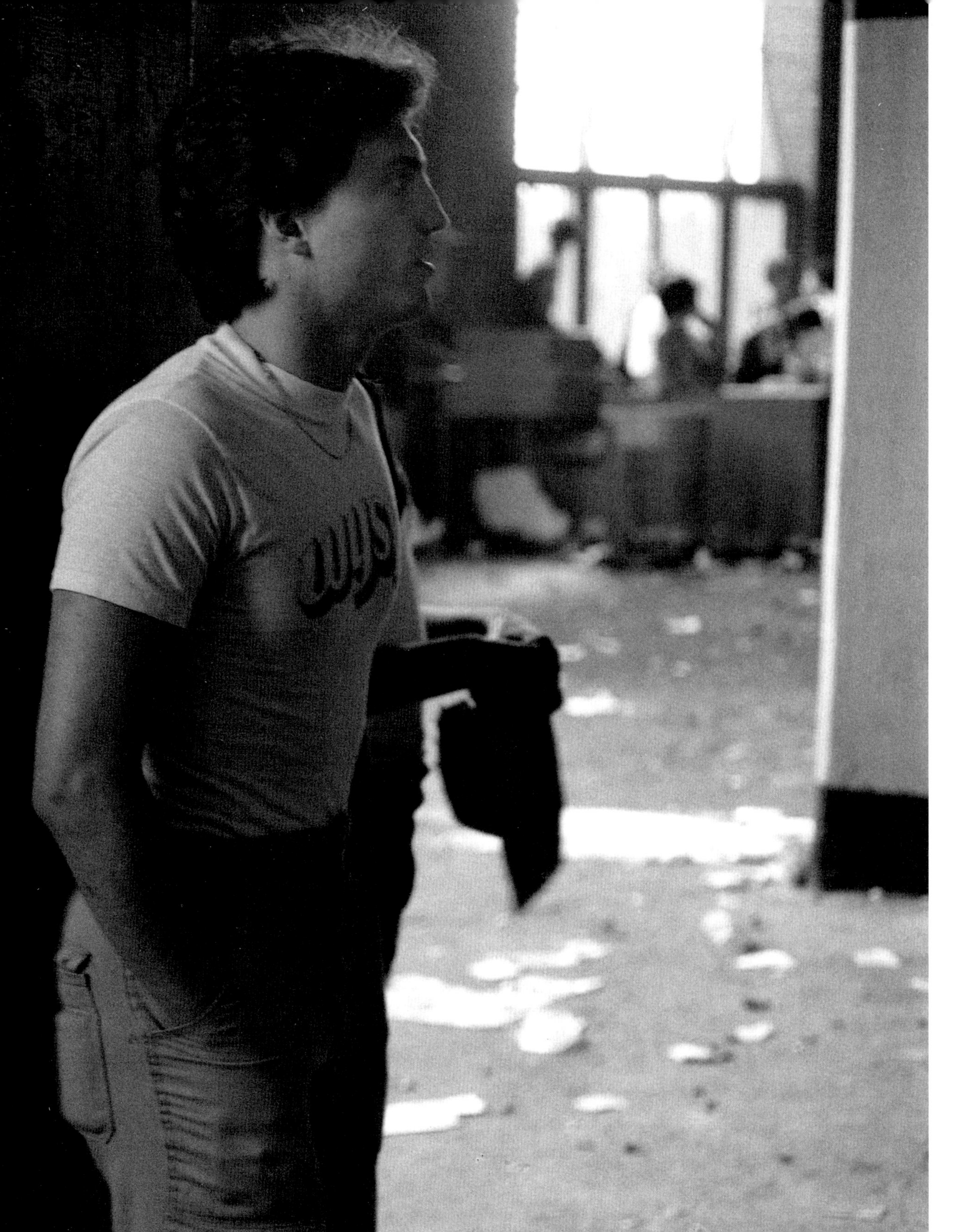

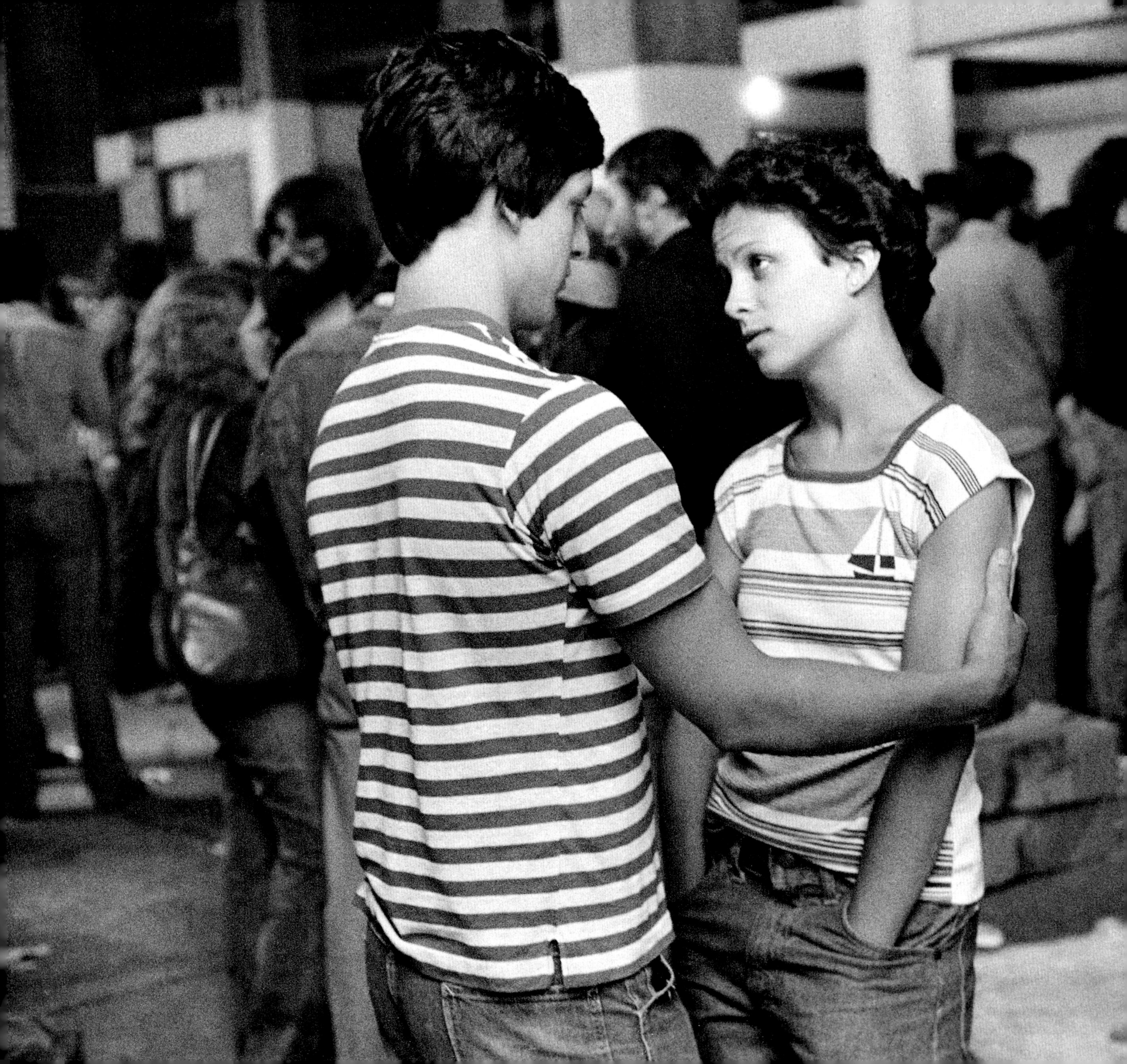

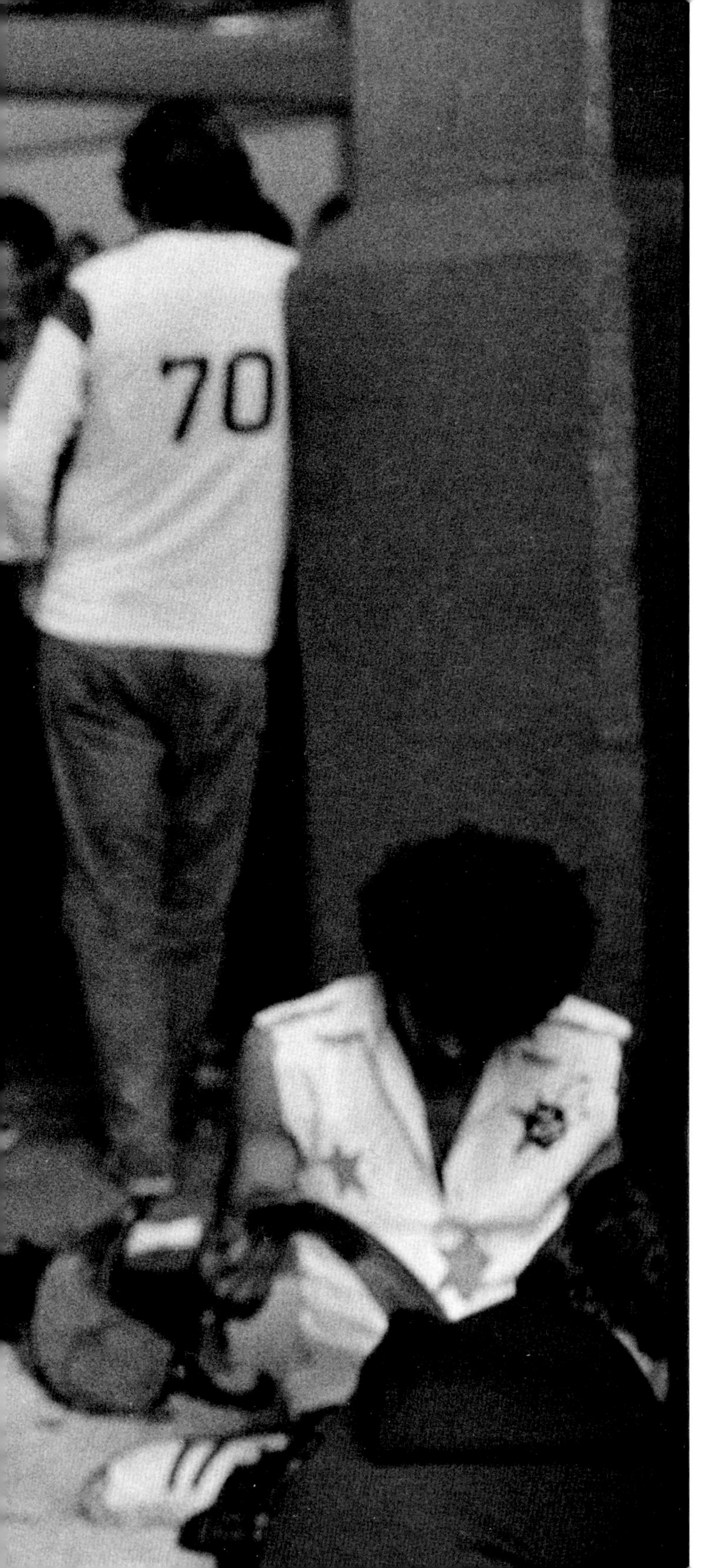

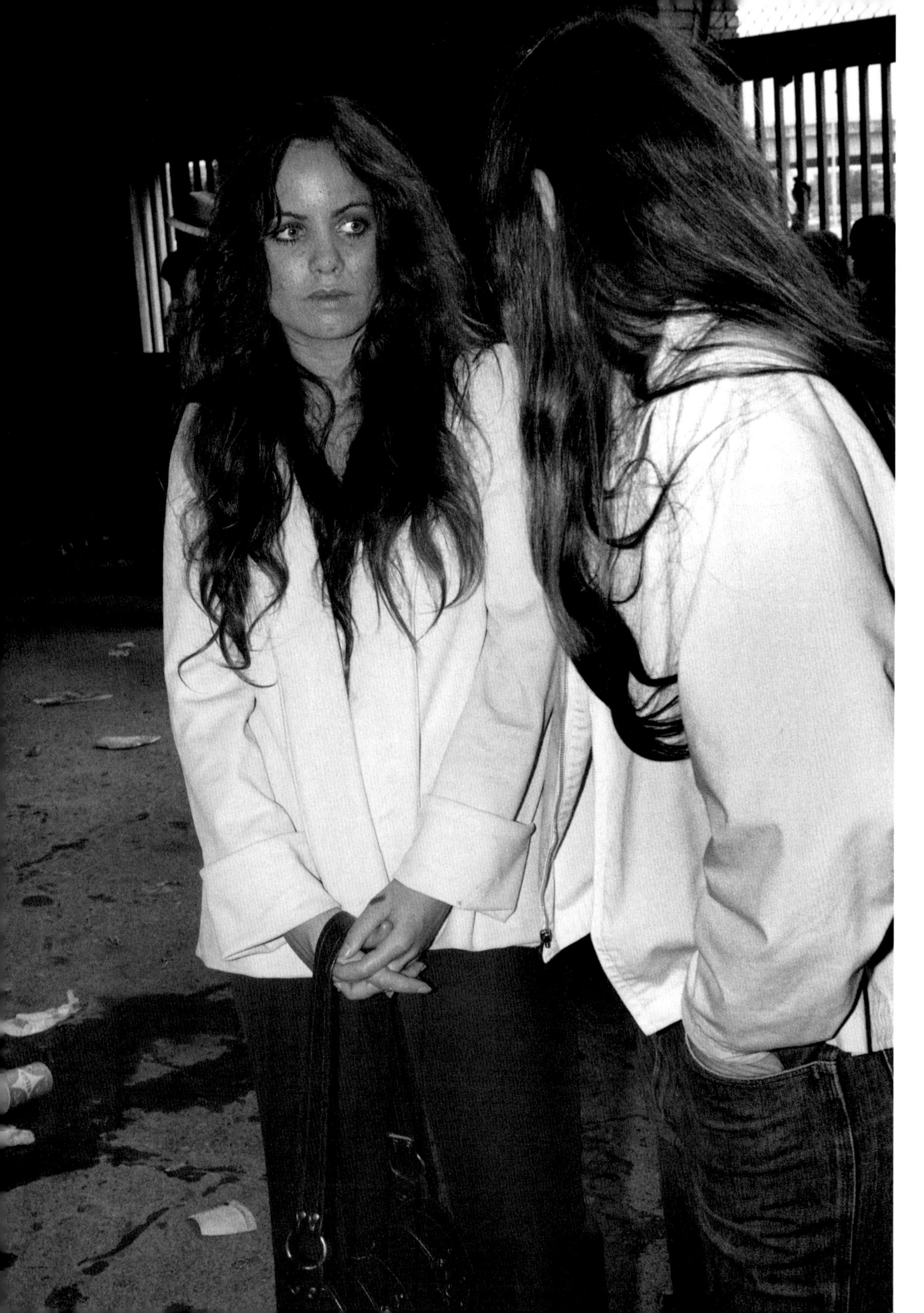

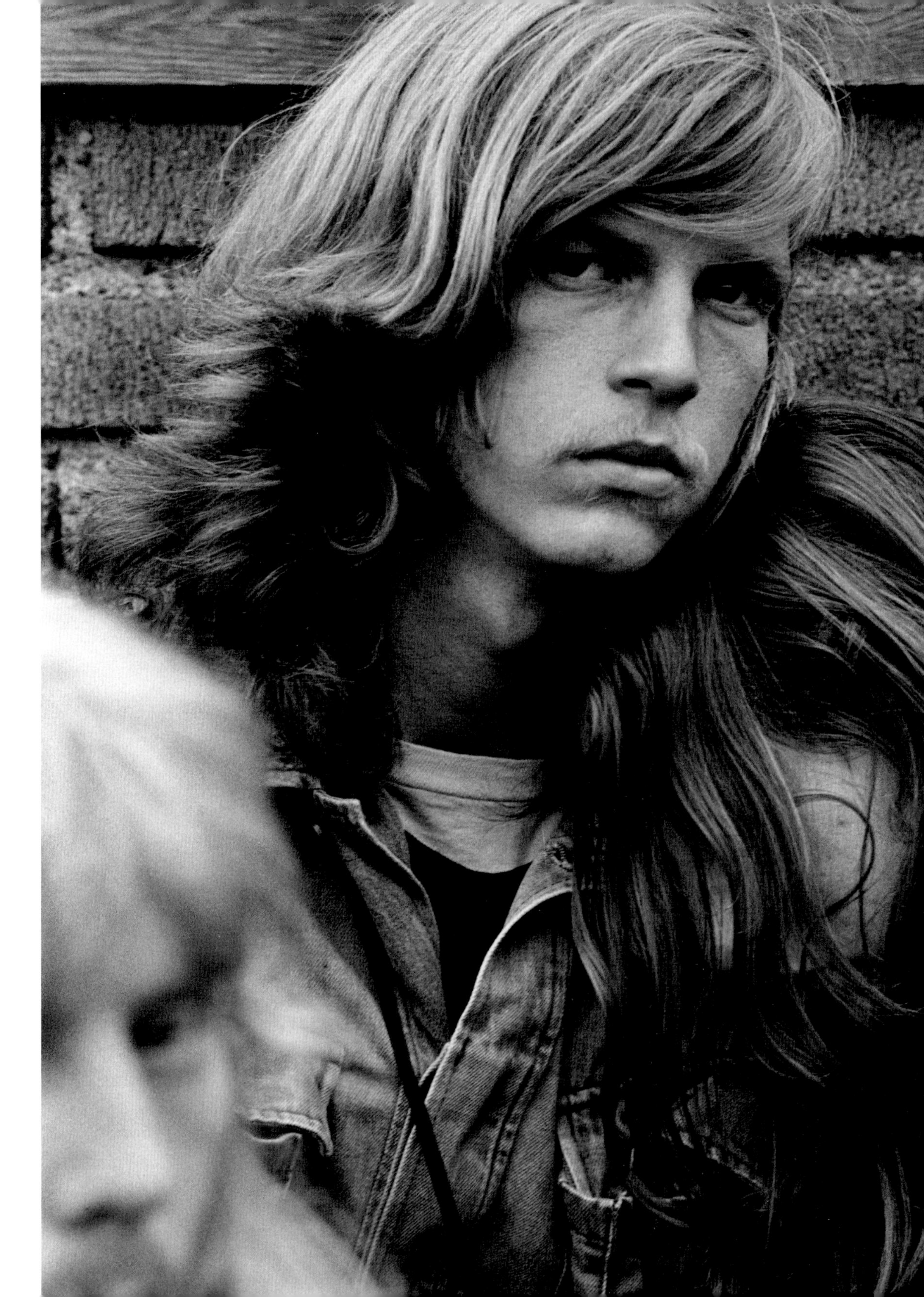

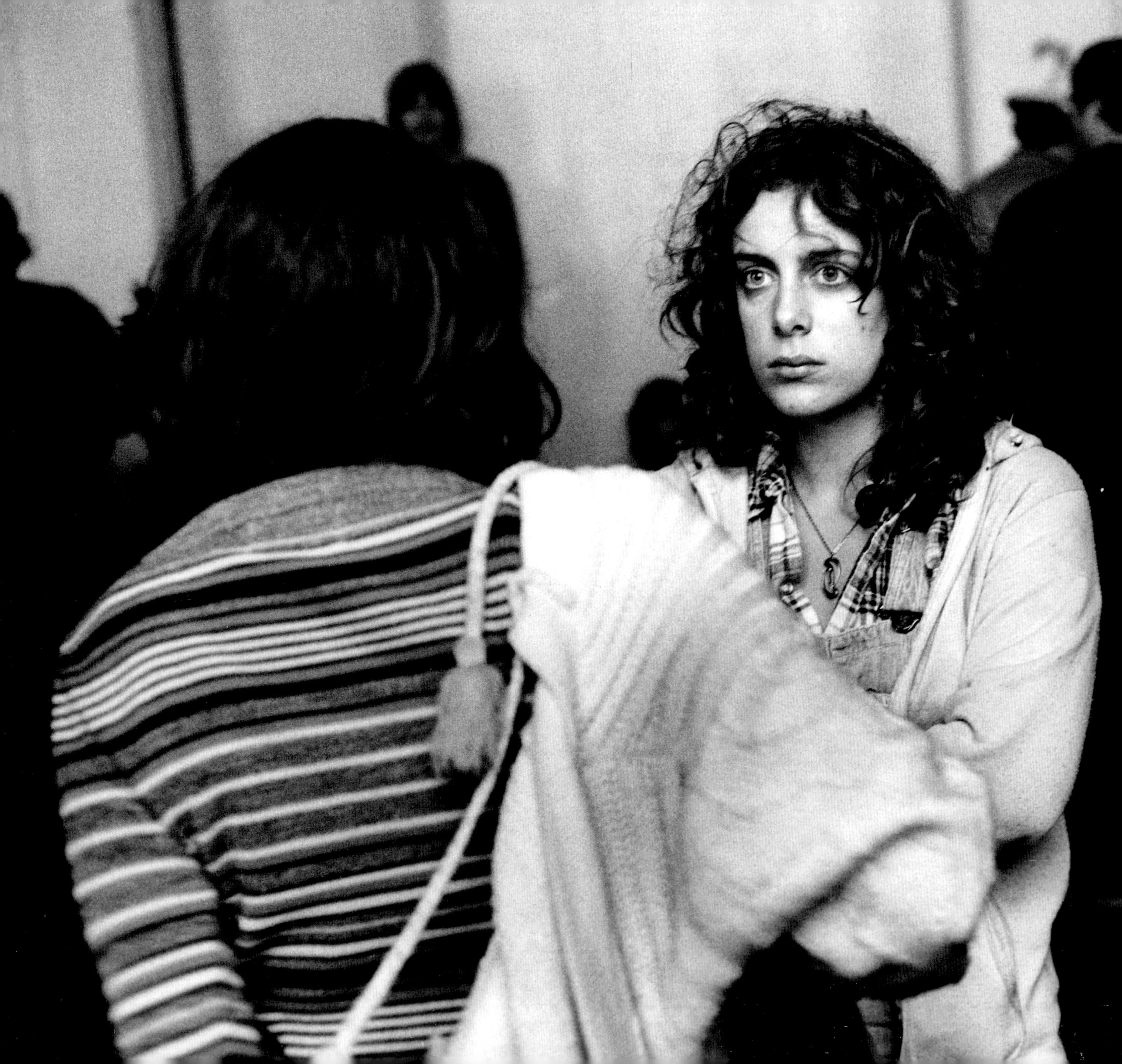

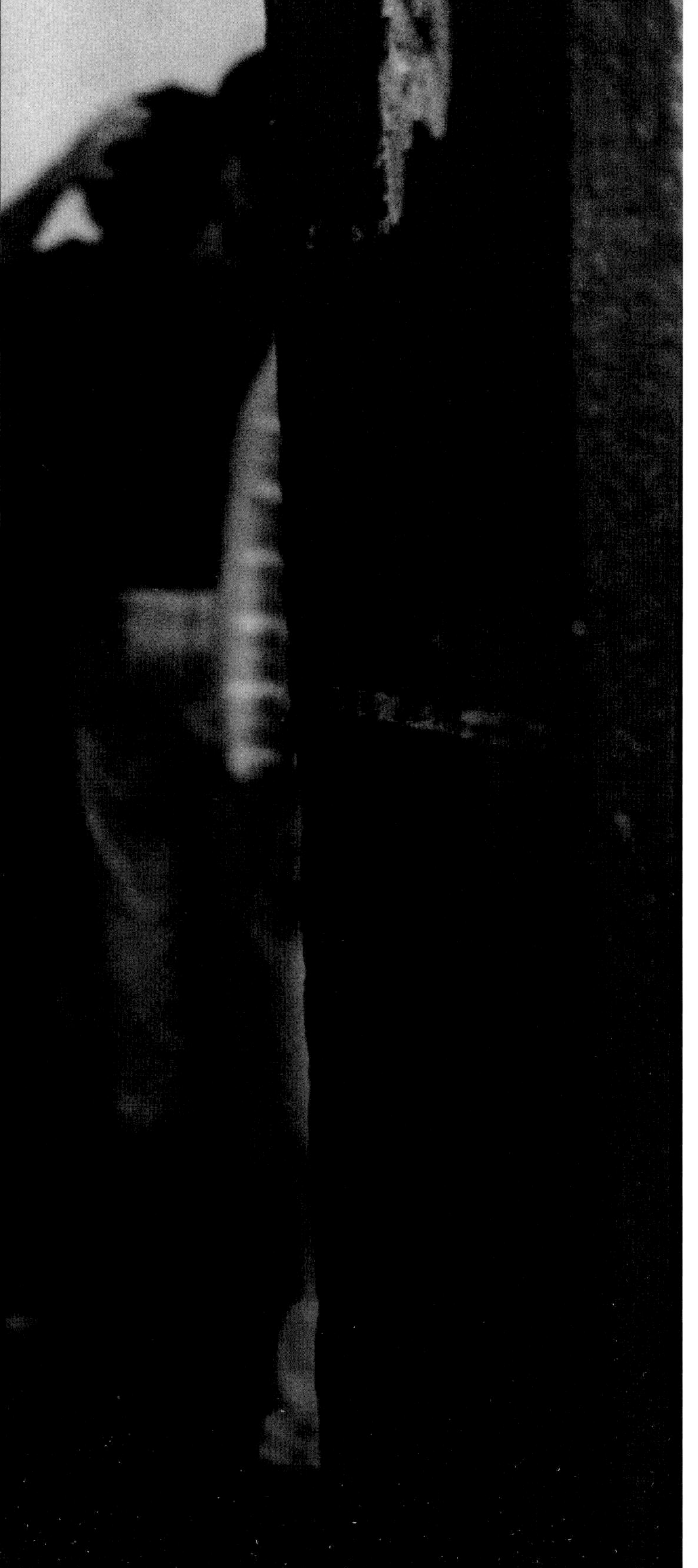

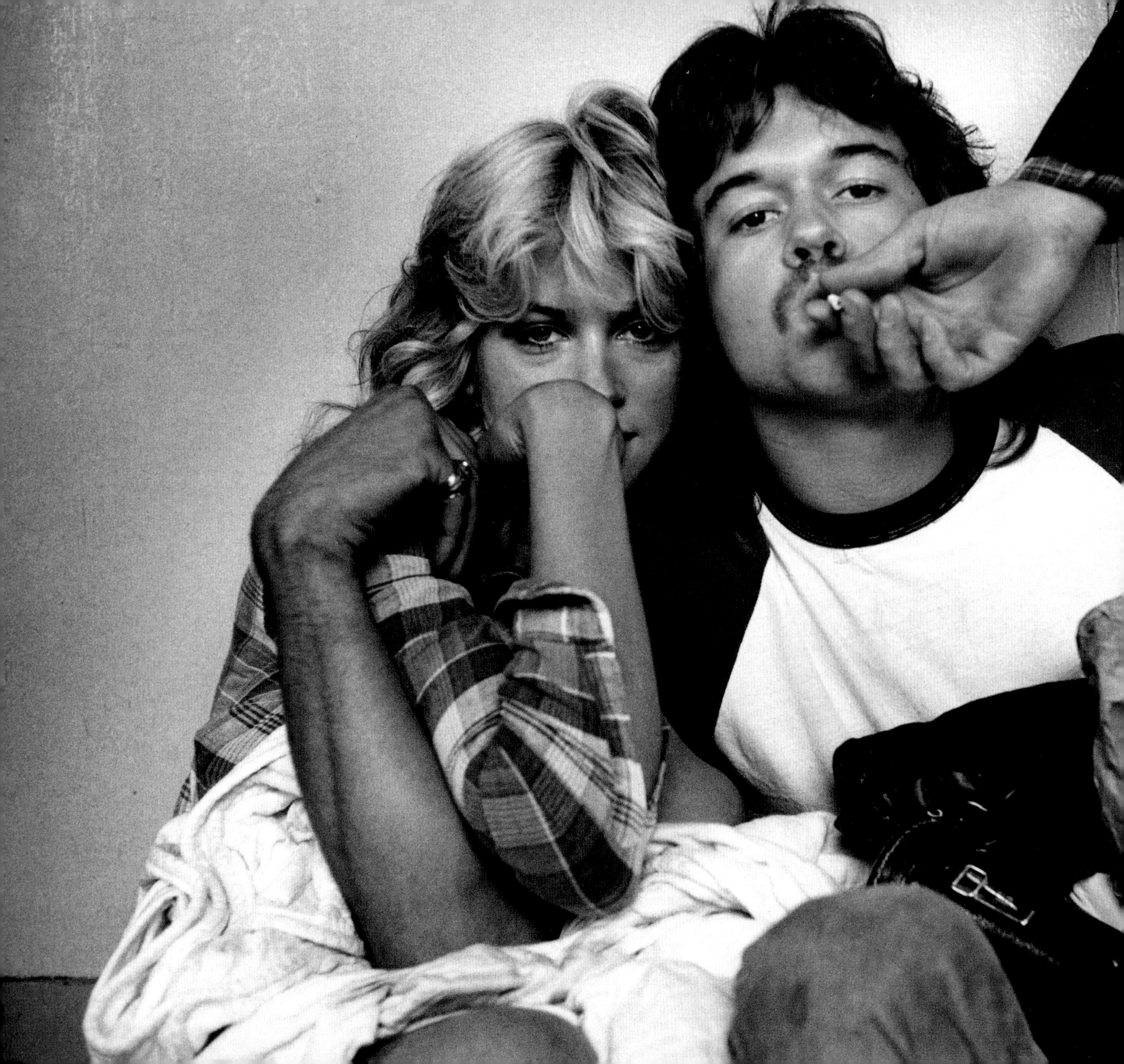

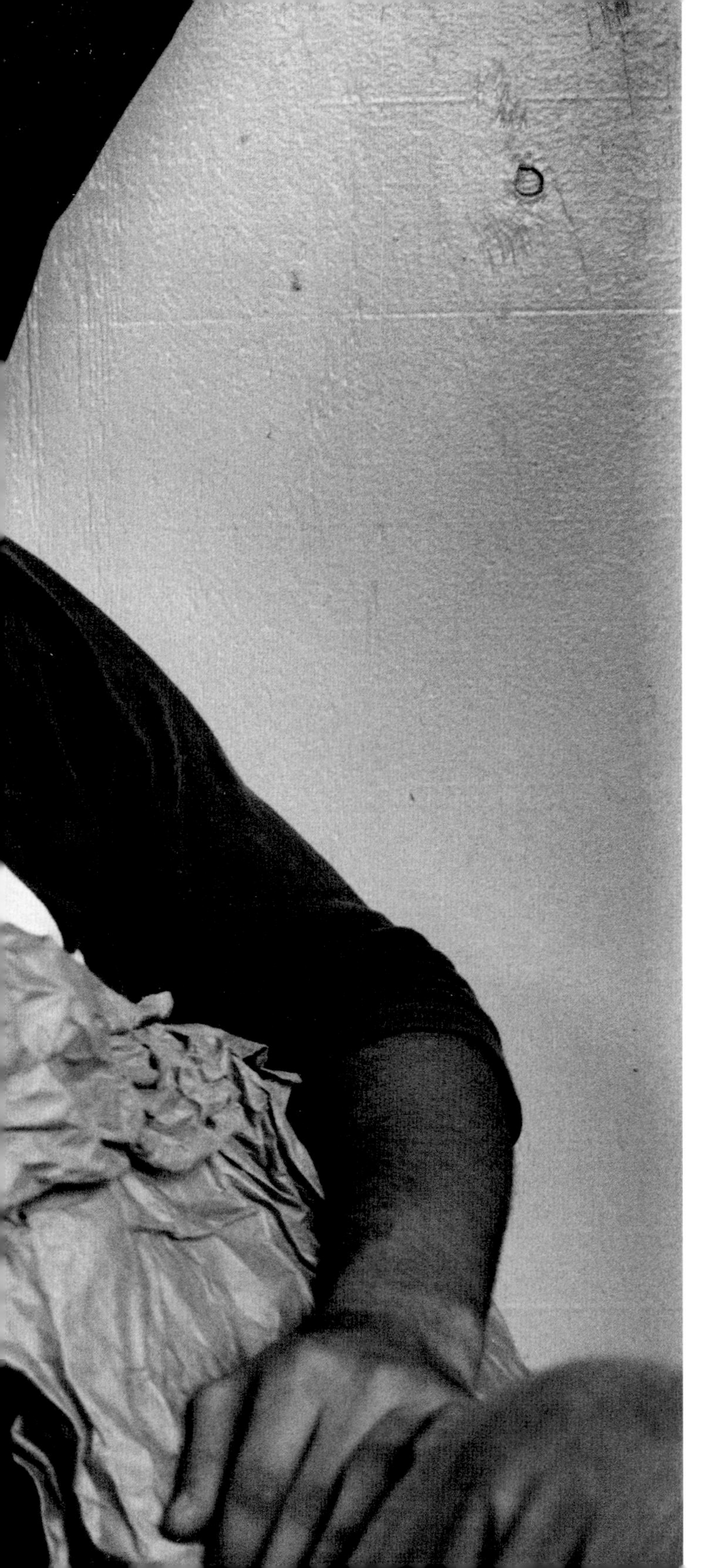

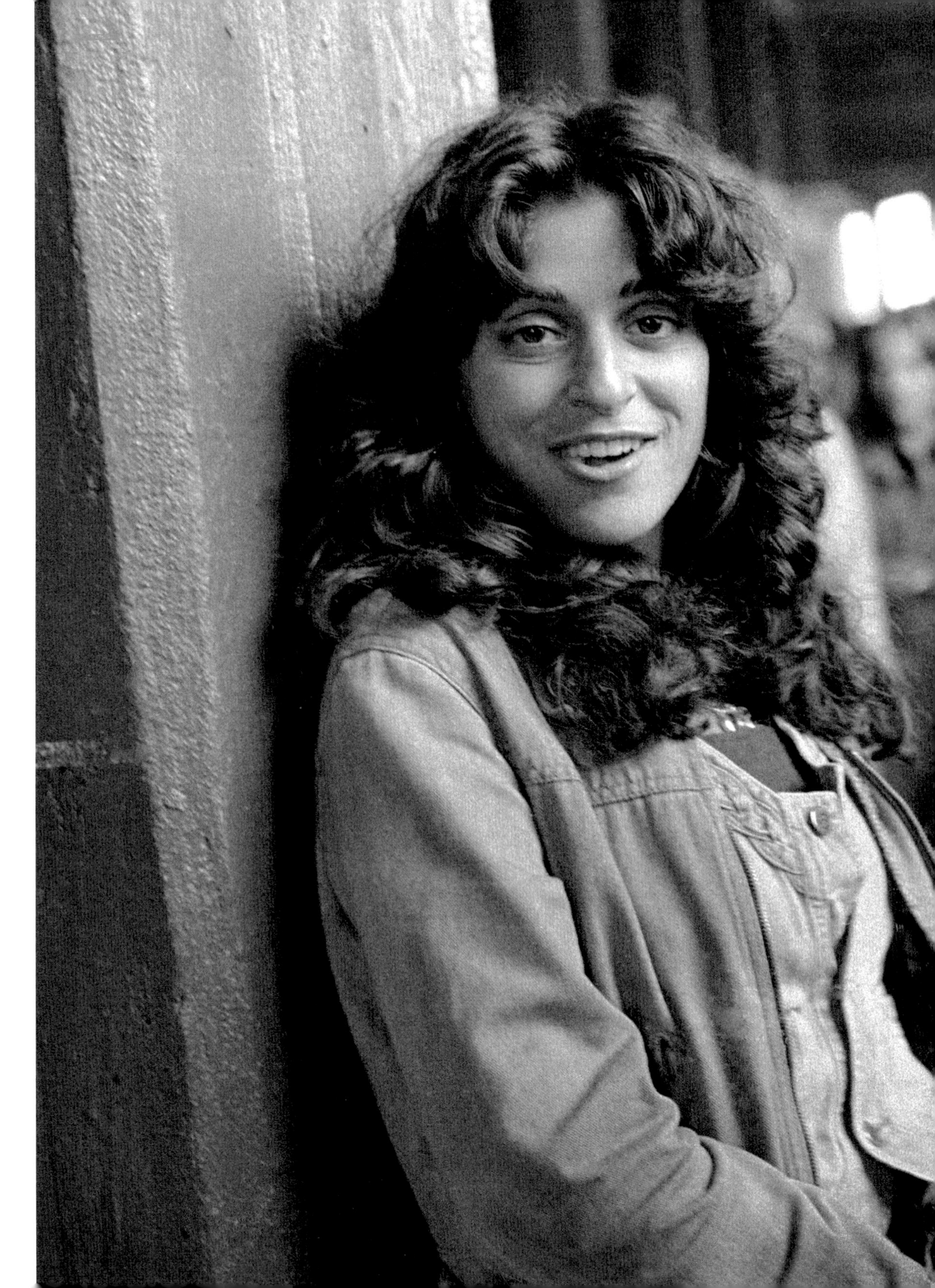

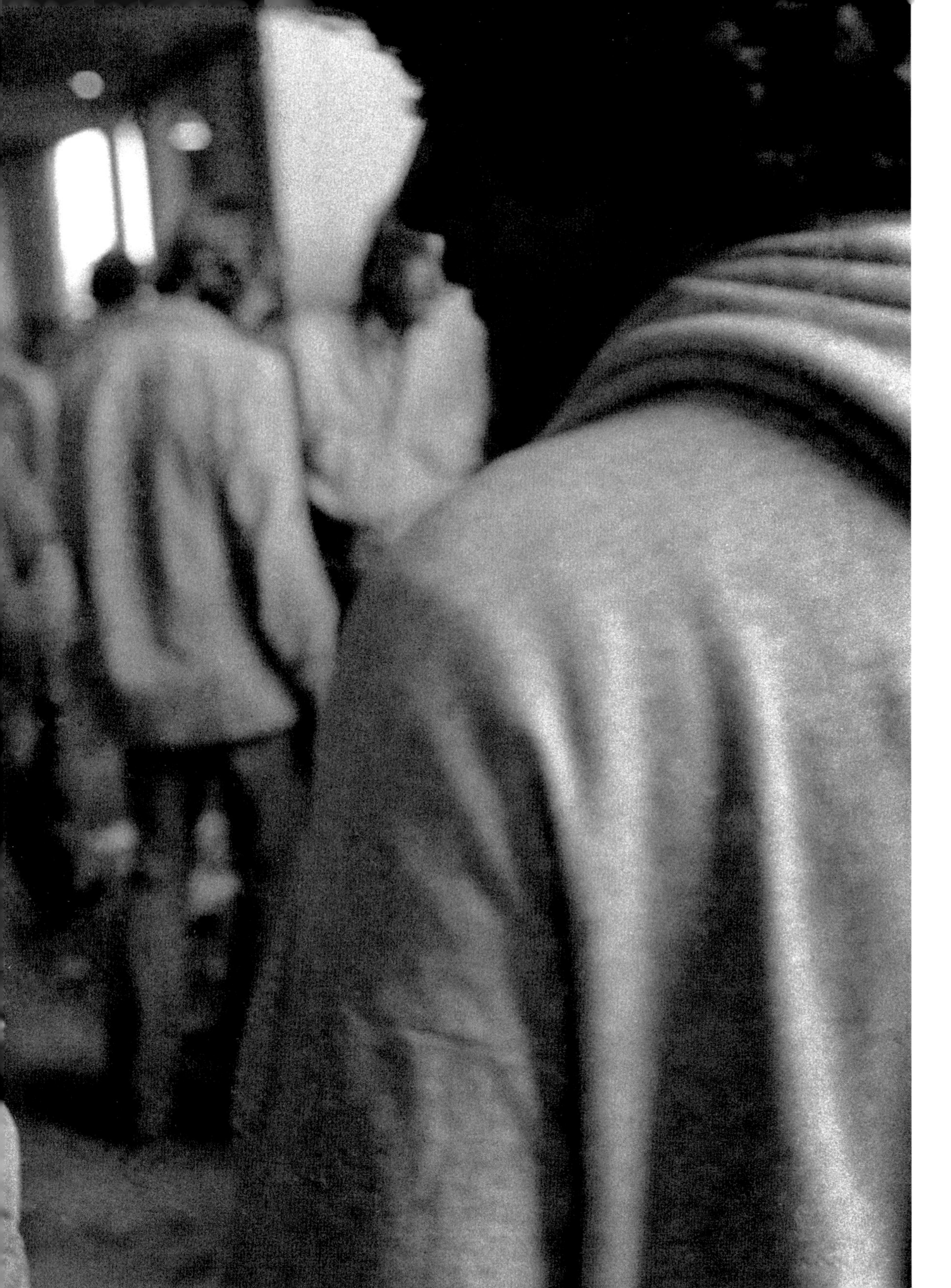

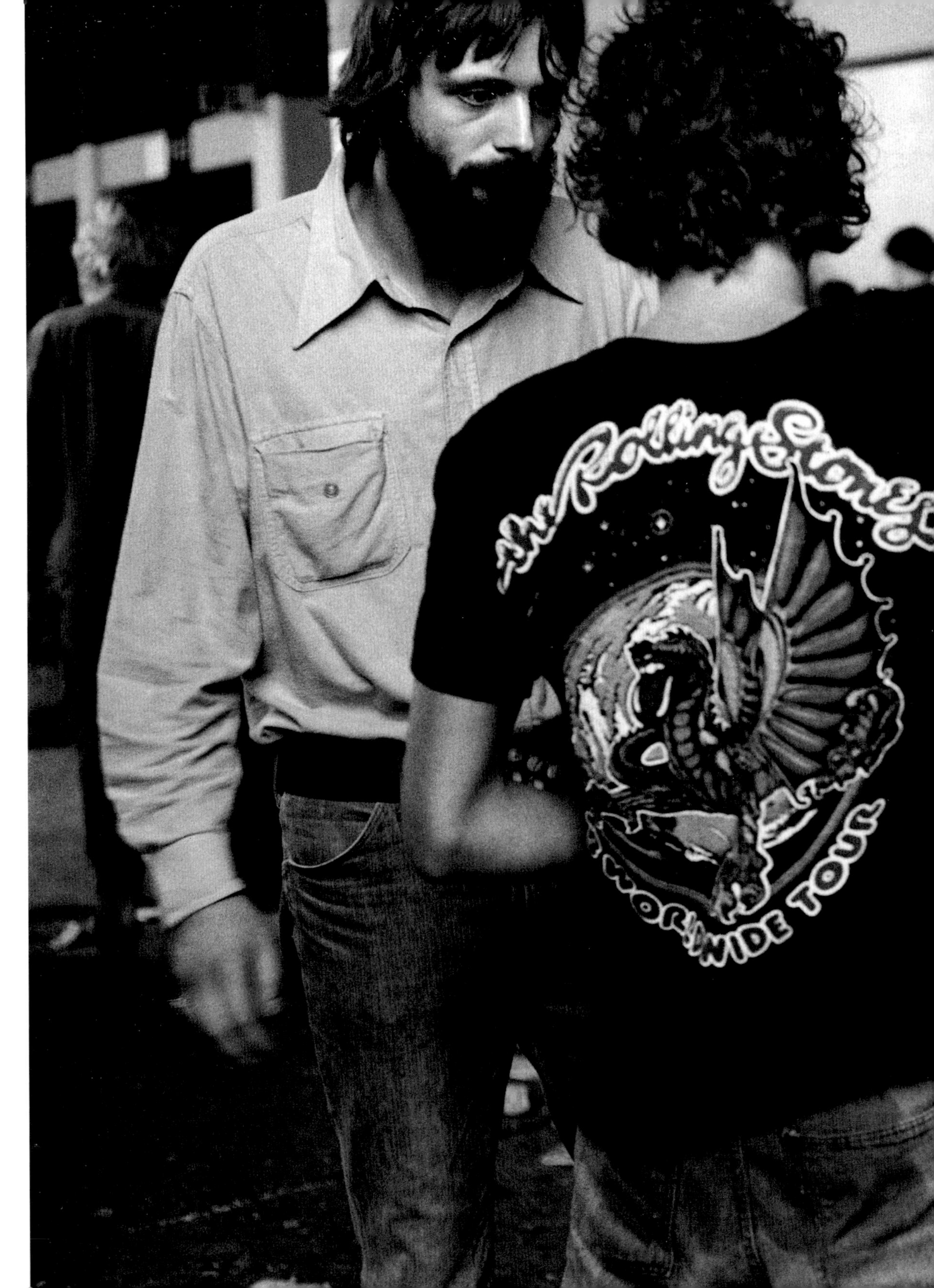

the Rolling Stones
WORLD WIDE TOUR

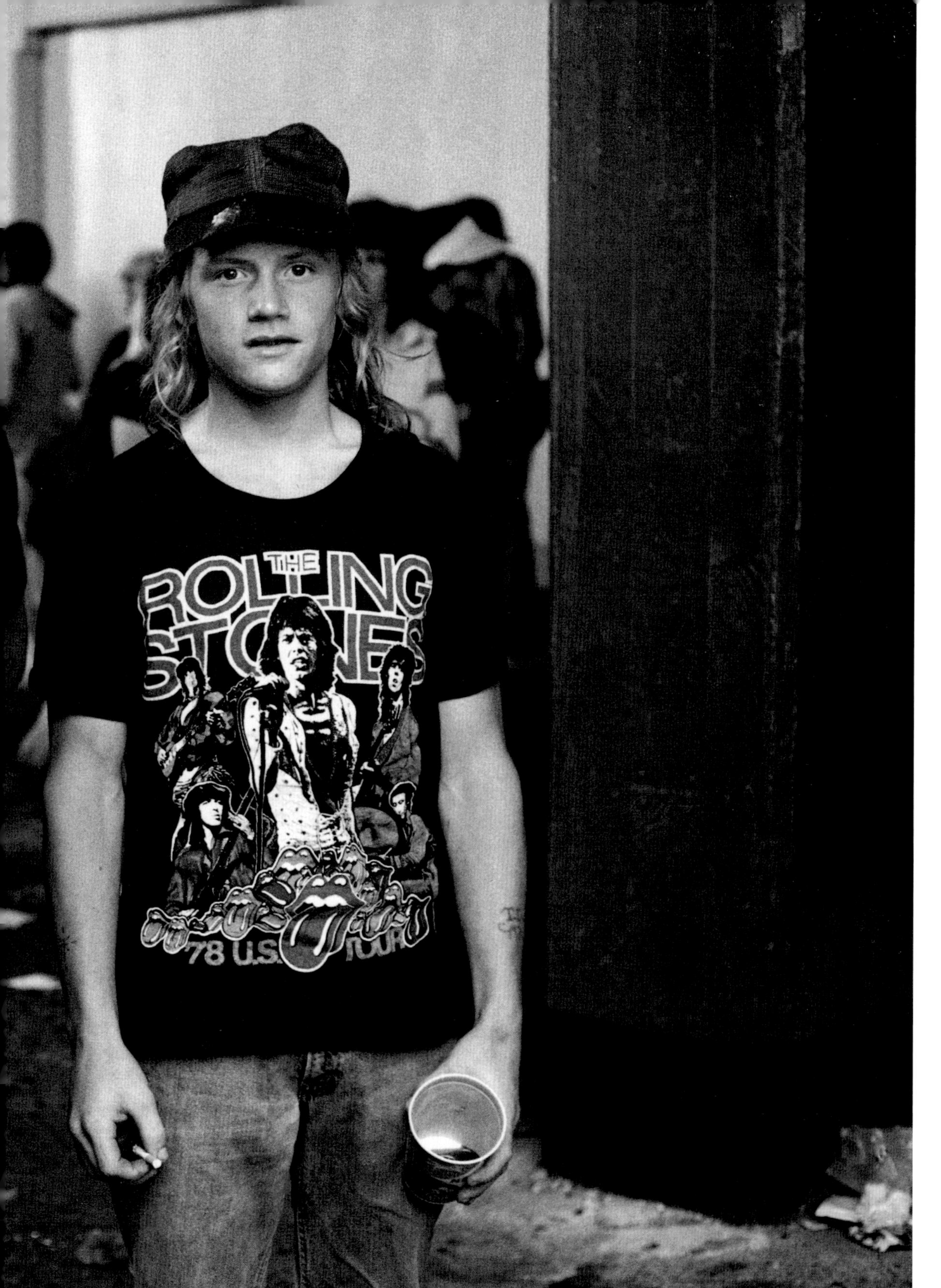
THE ROLLING STONES
'78 U.S. TOUR

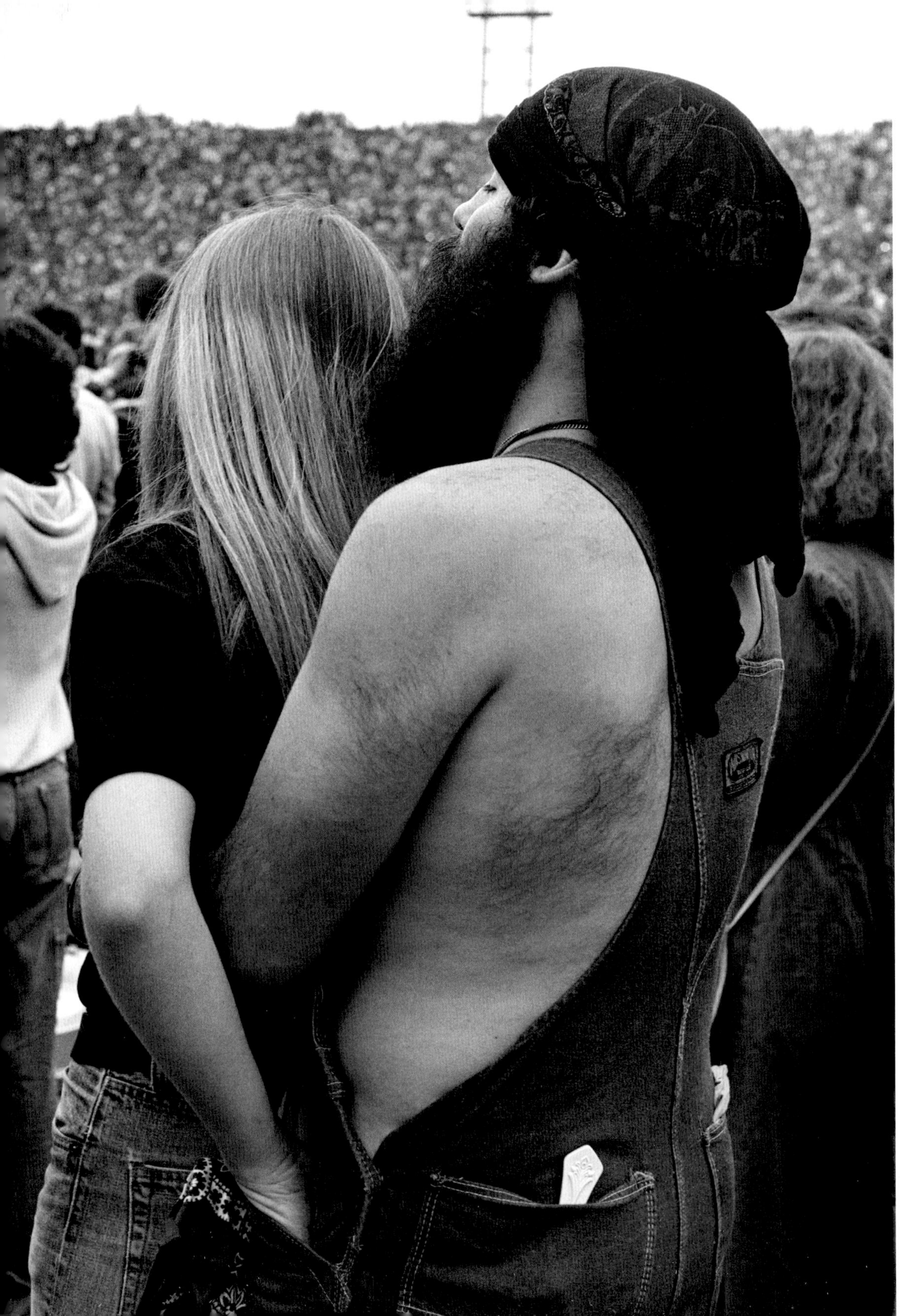

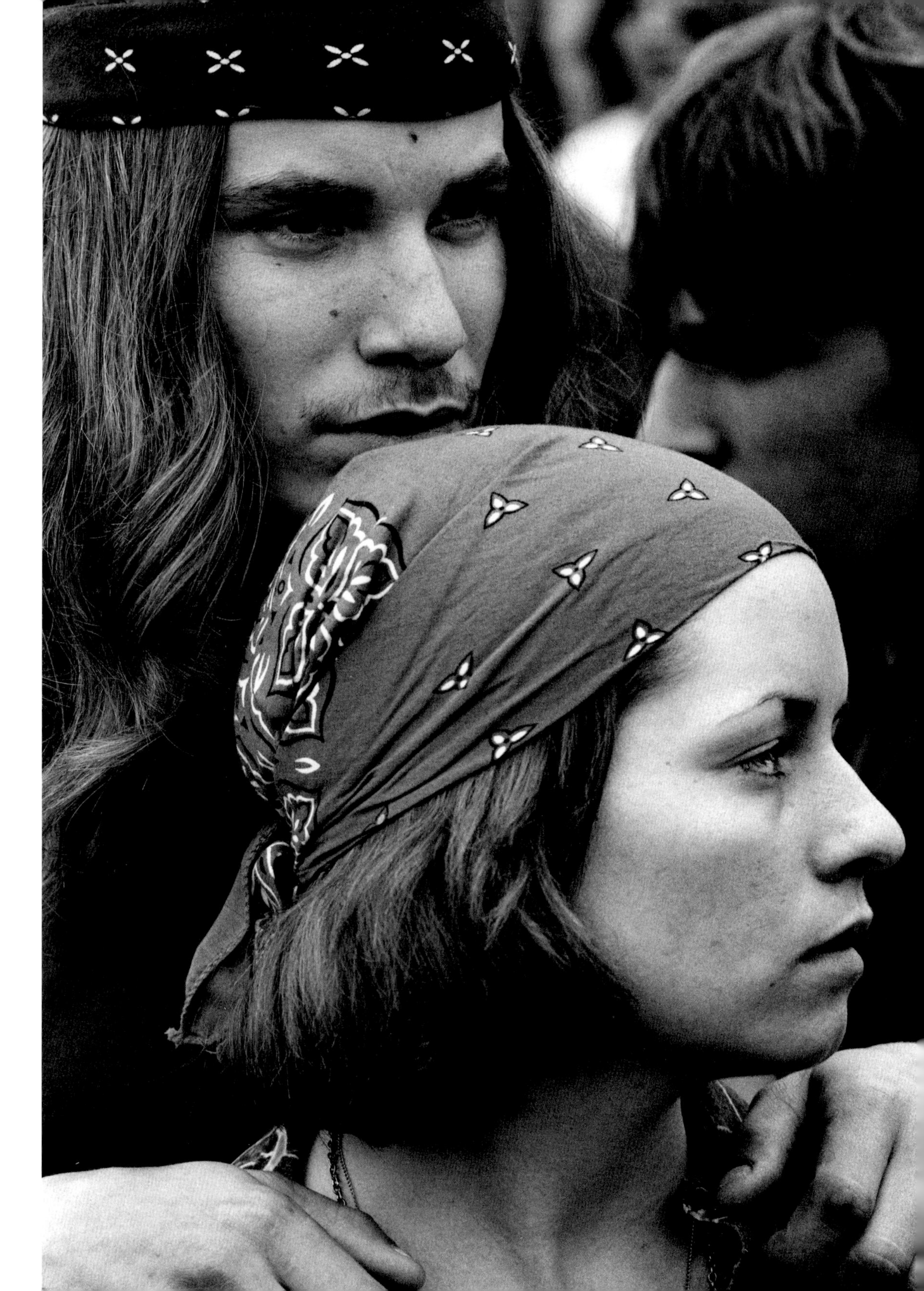

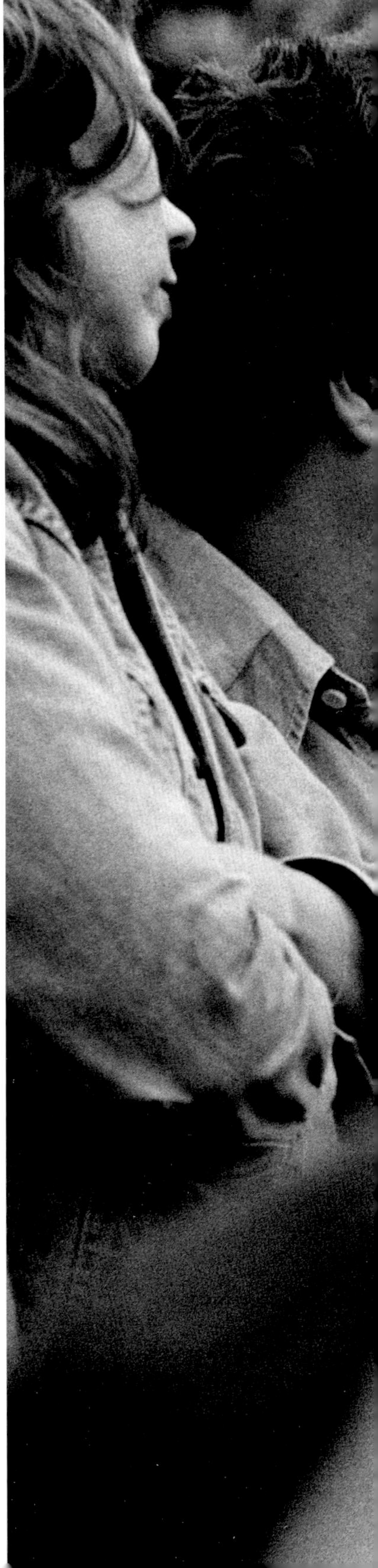

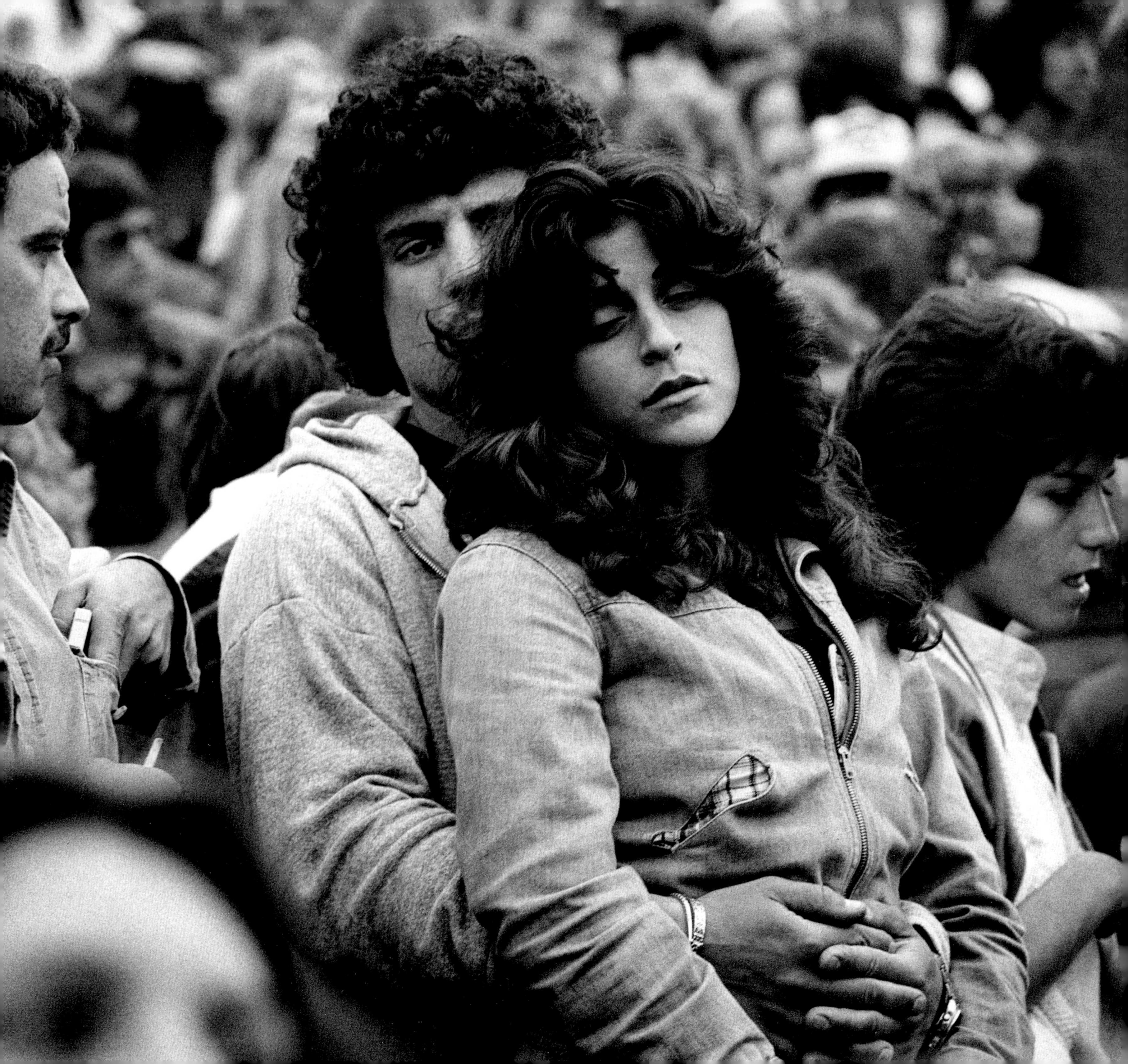

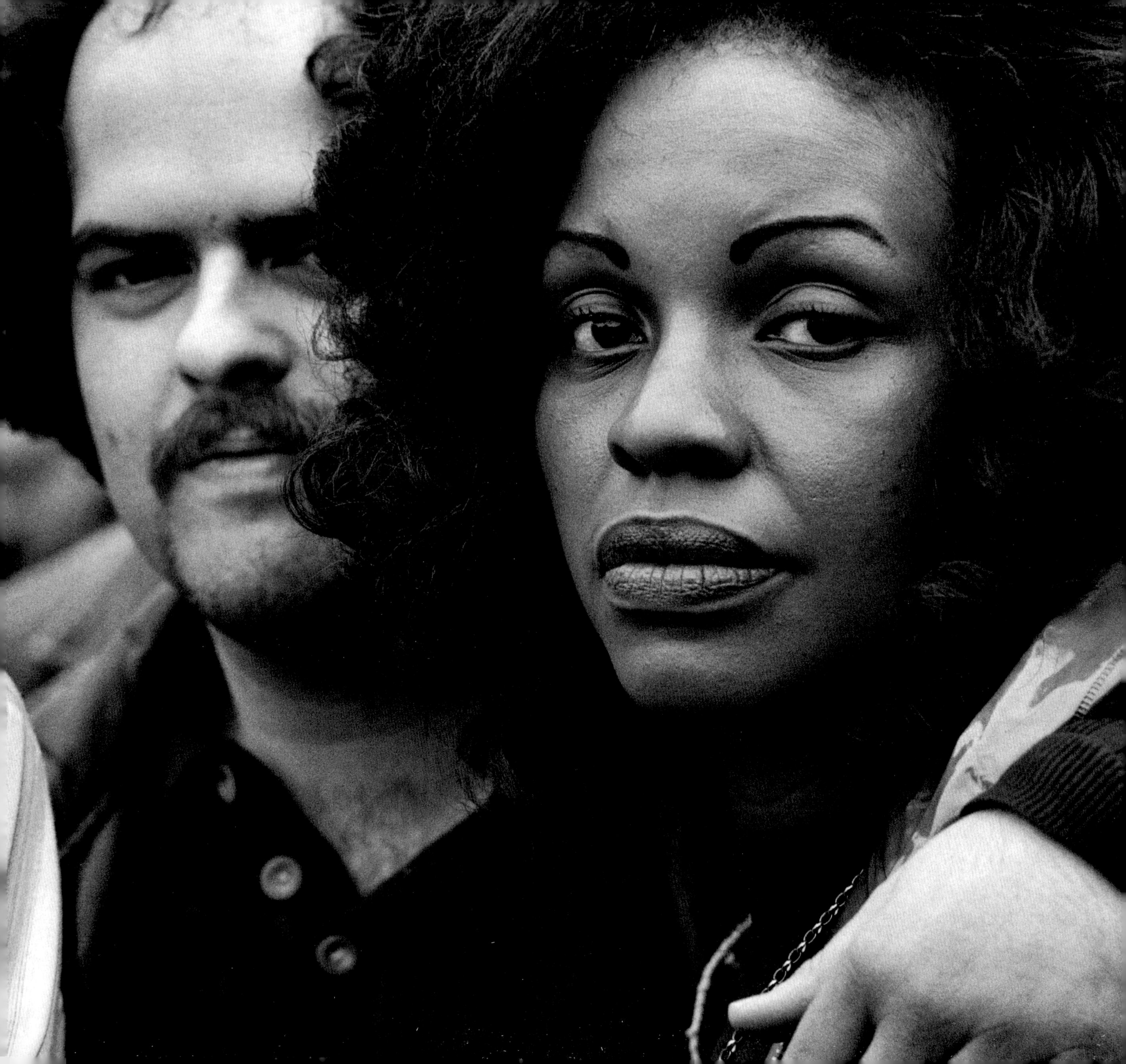

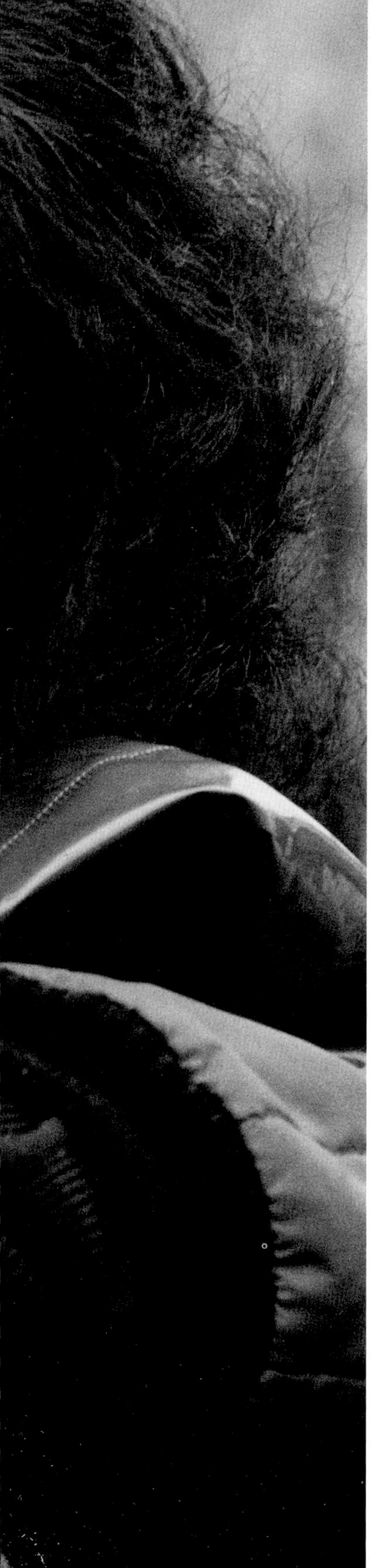

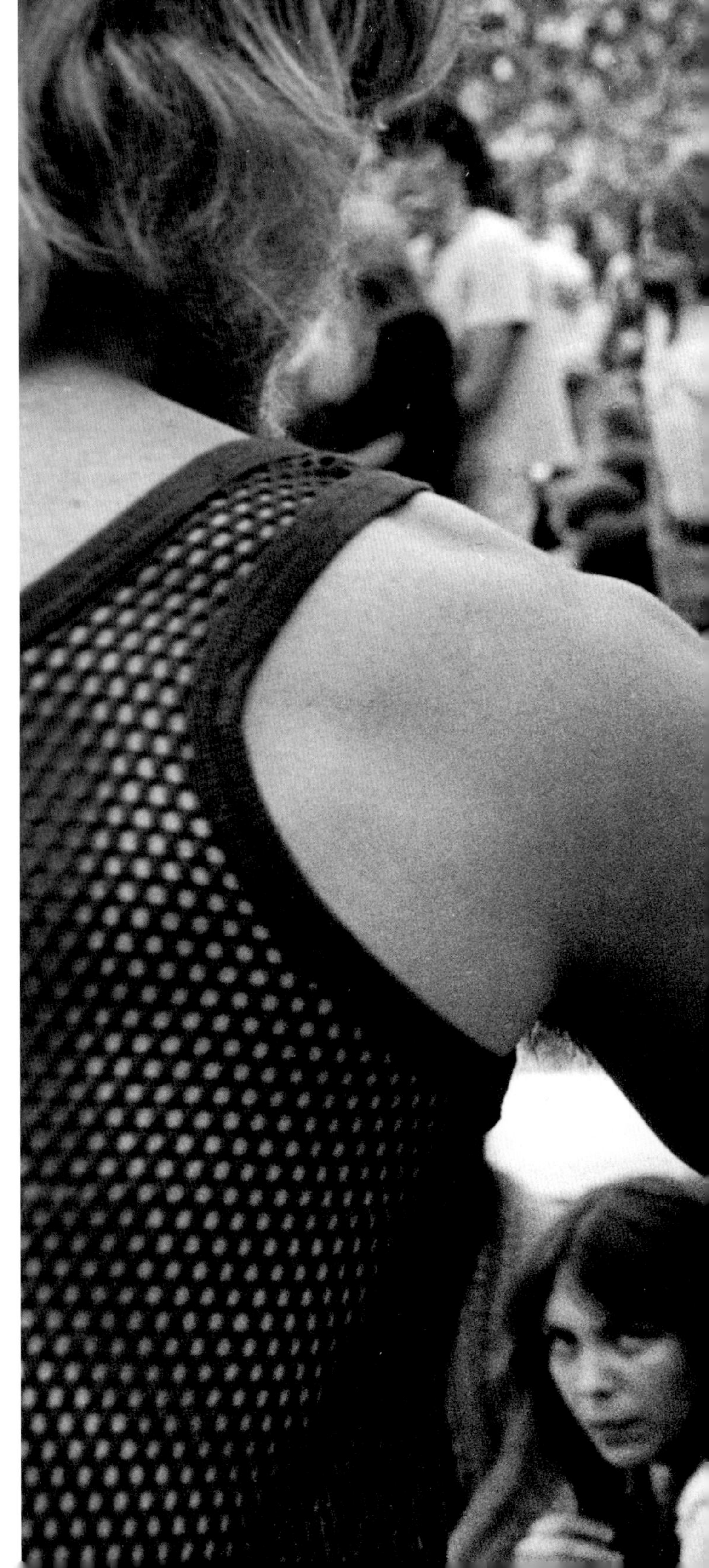

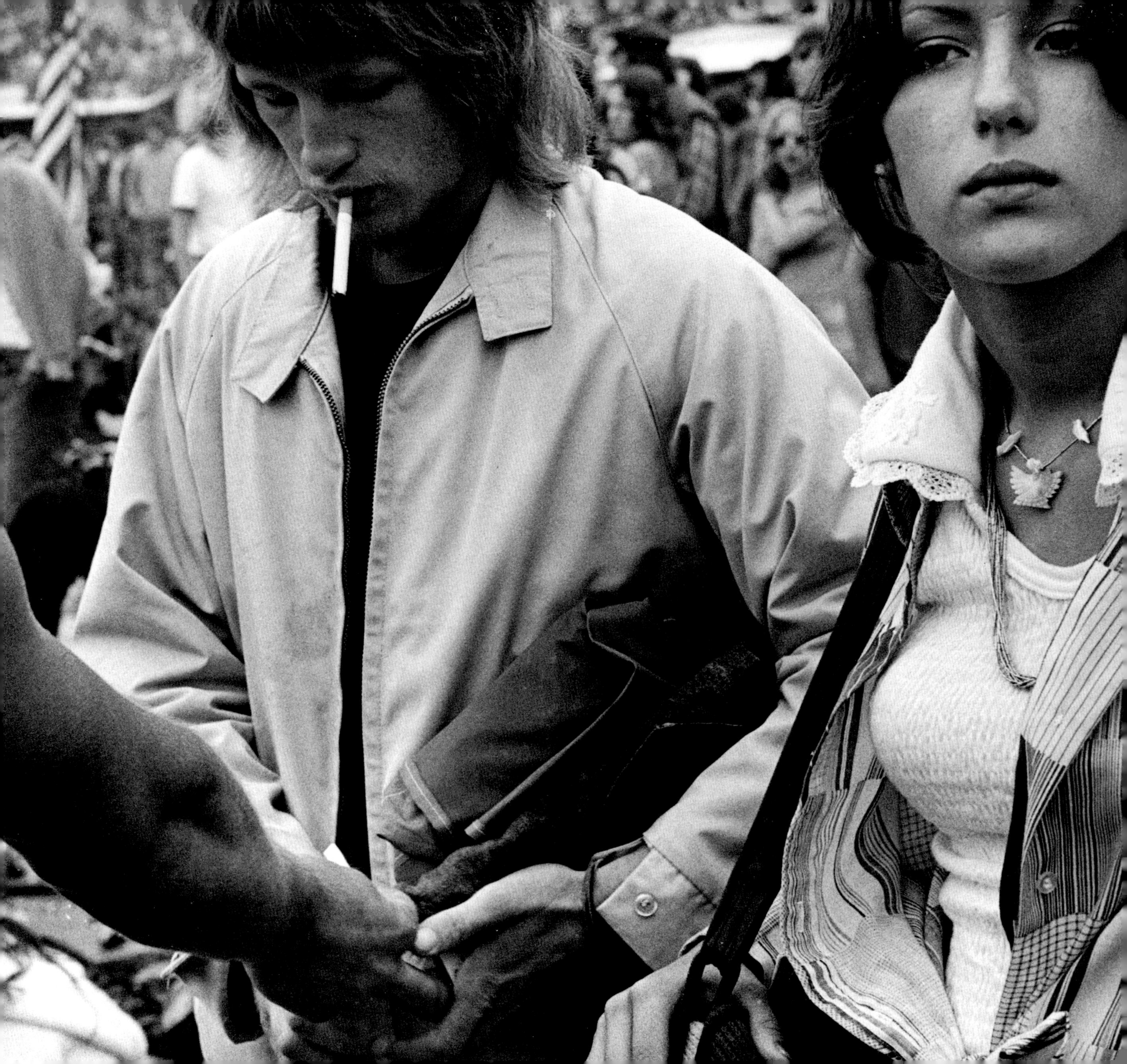

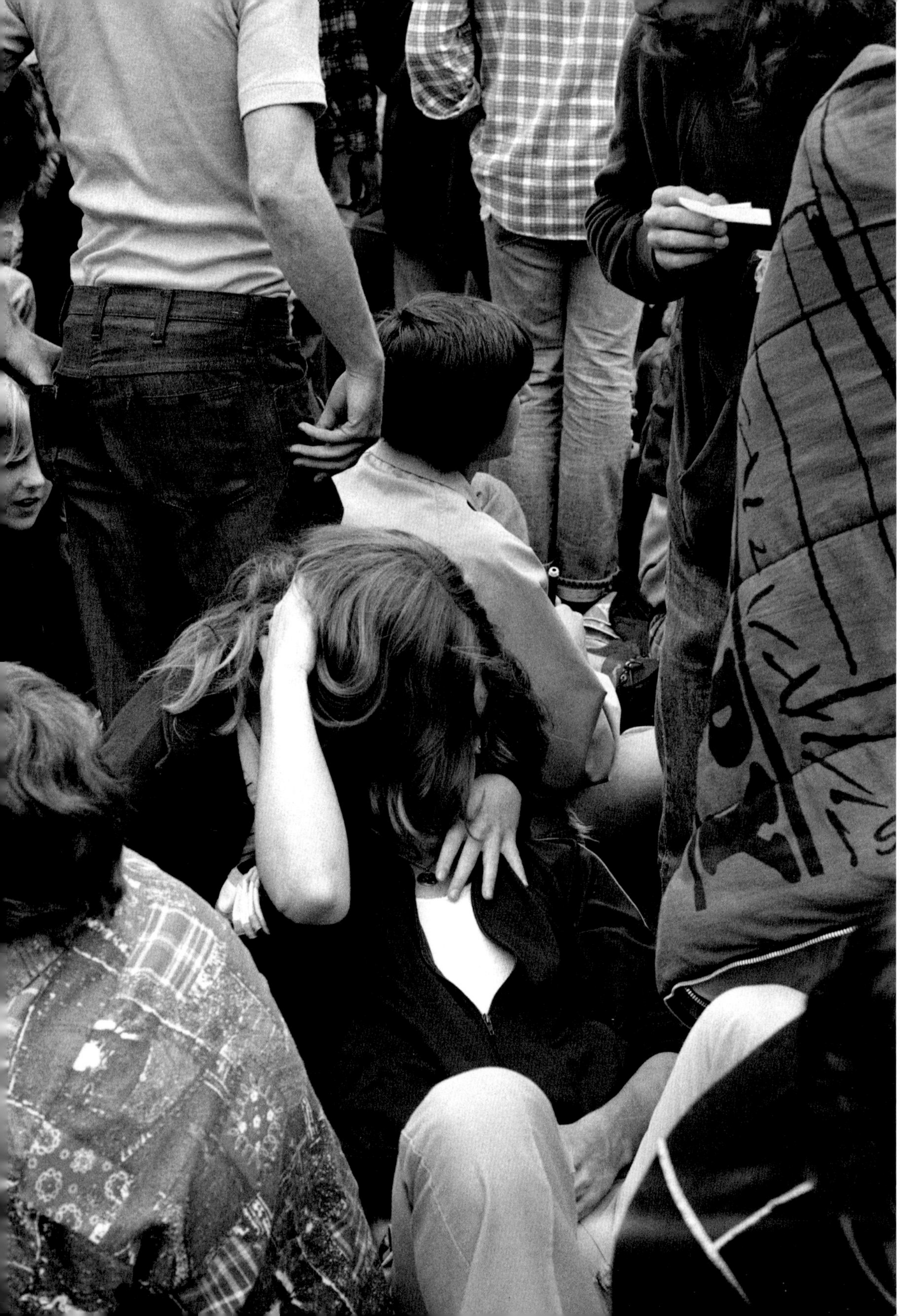

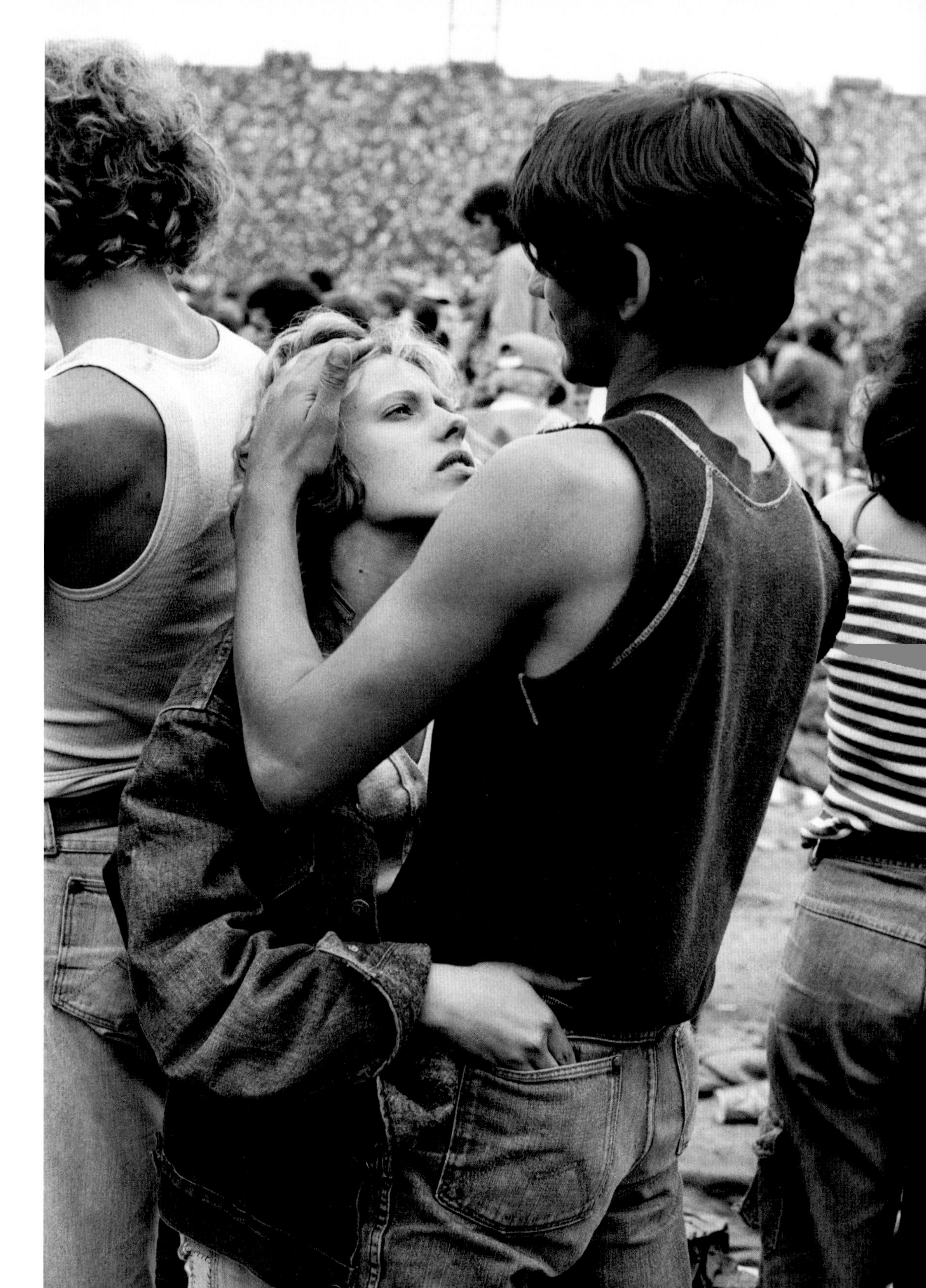

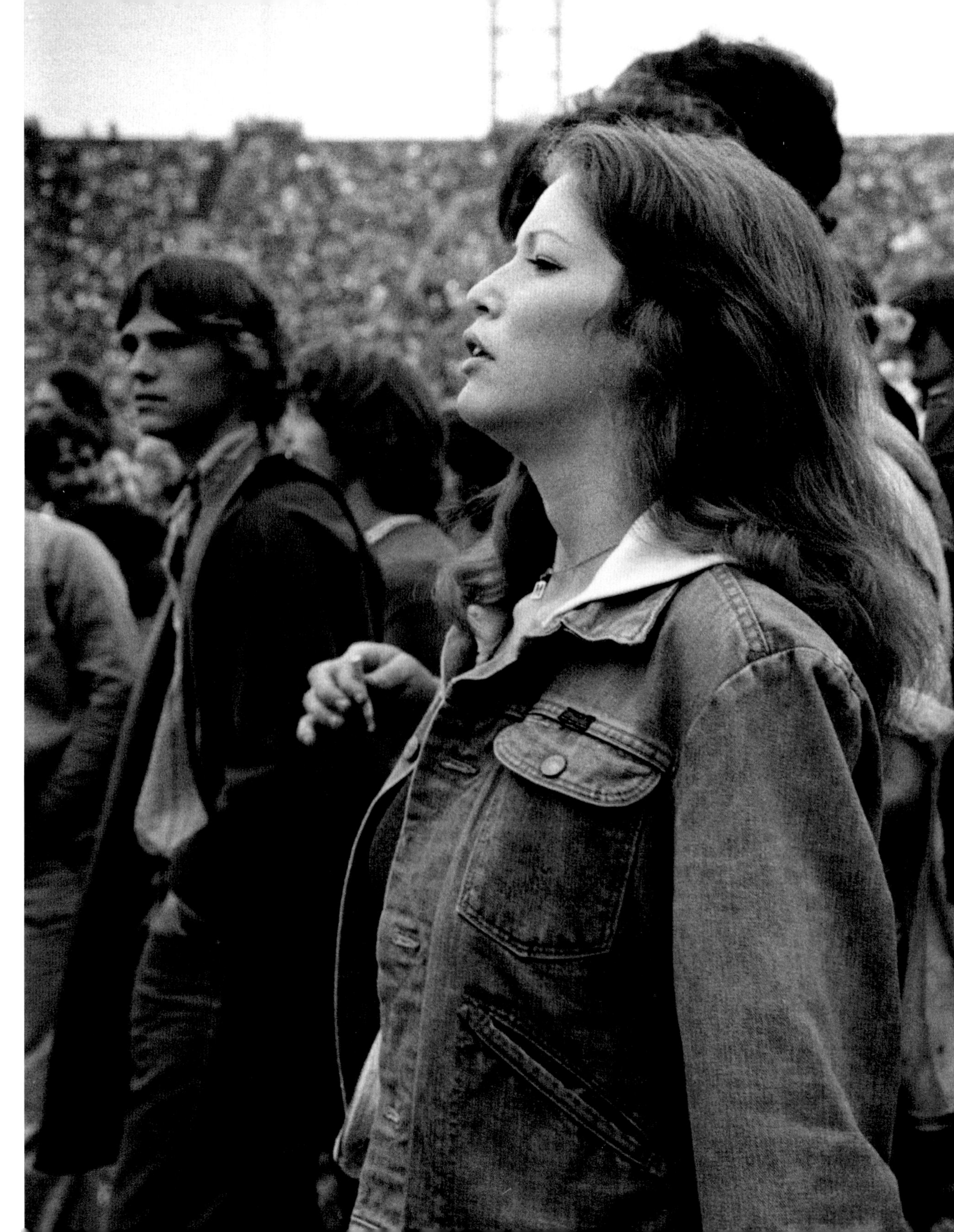

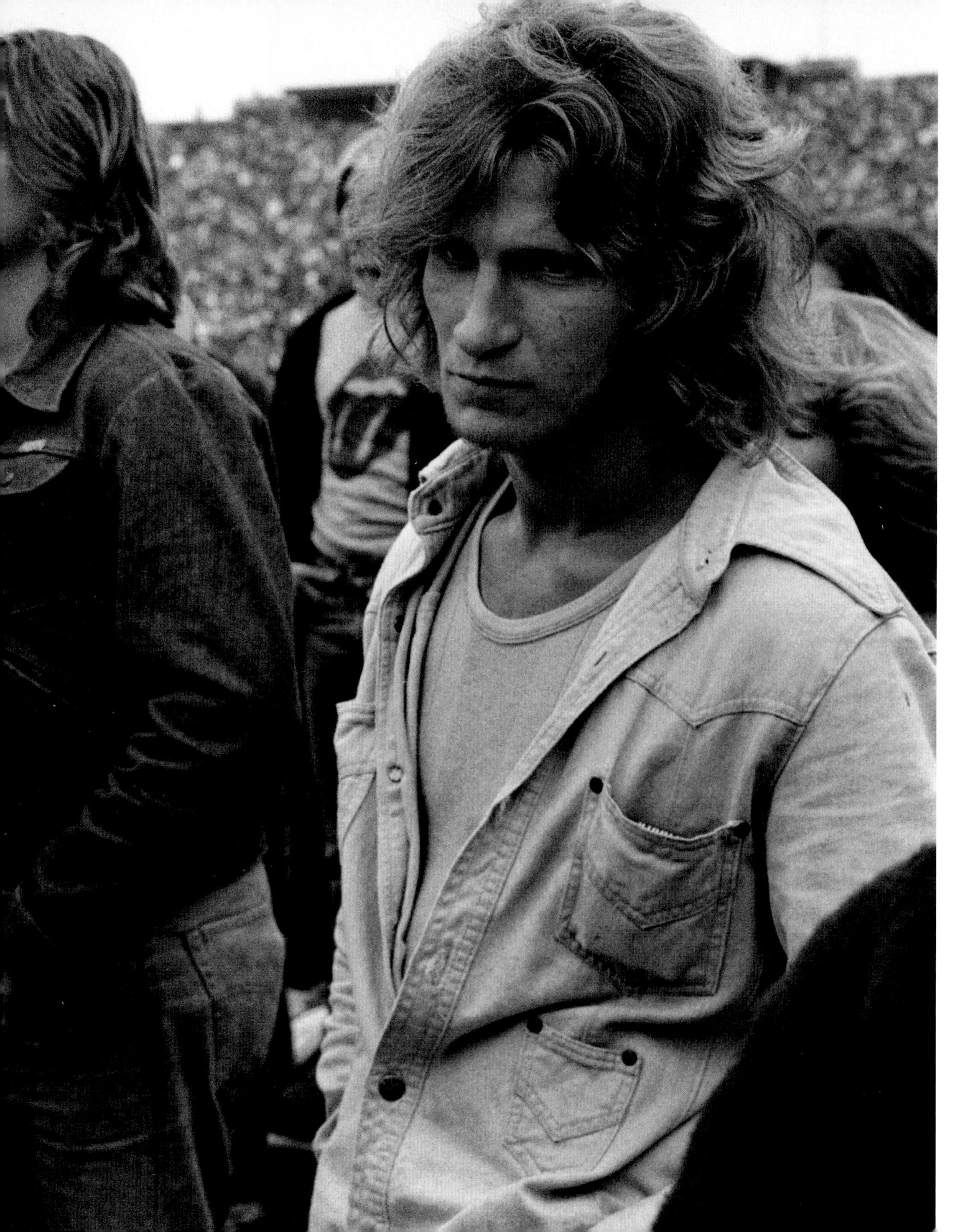

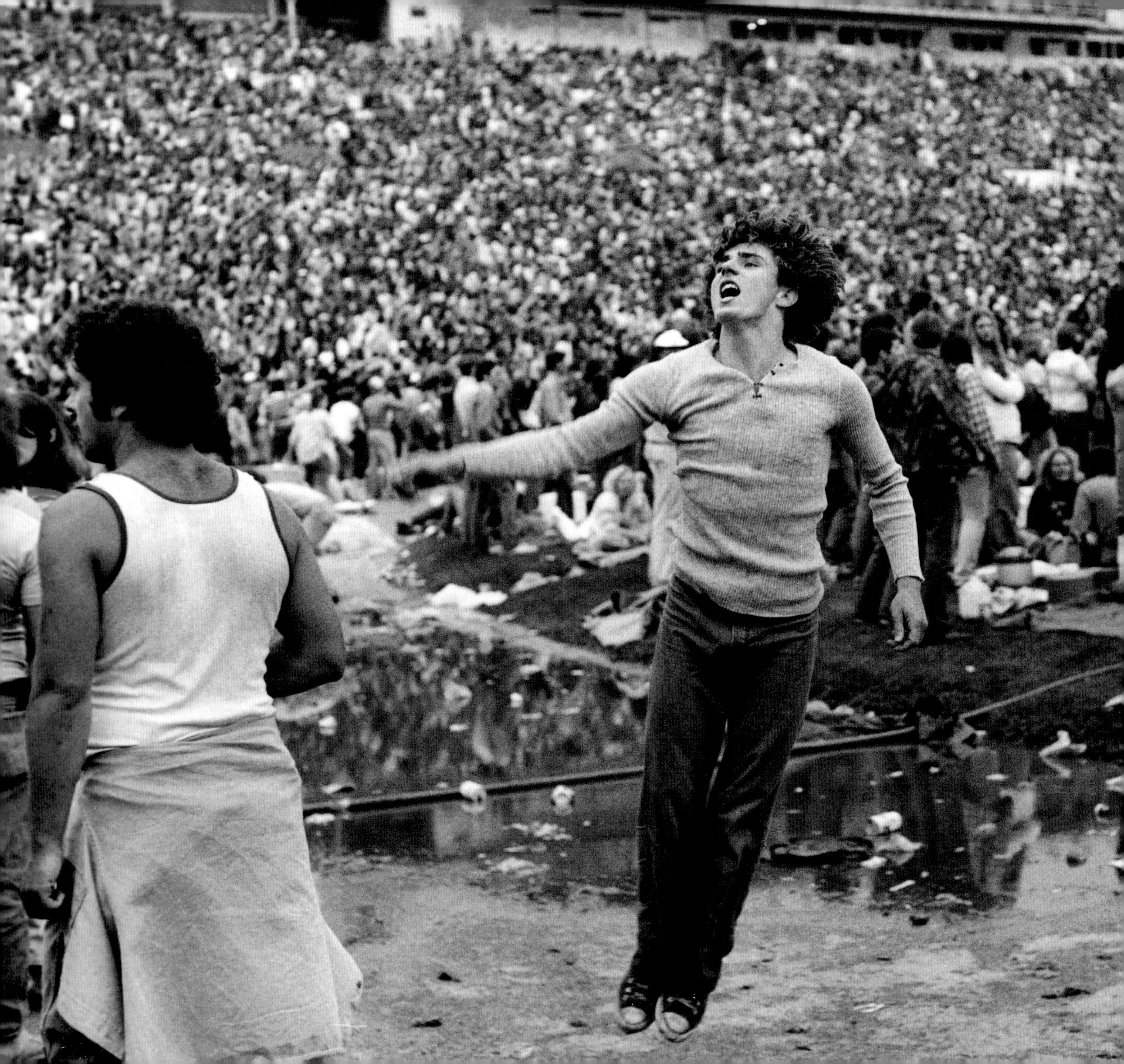

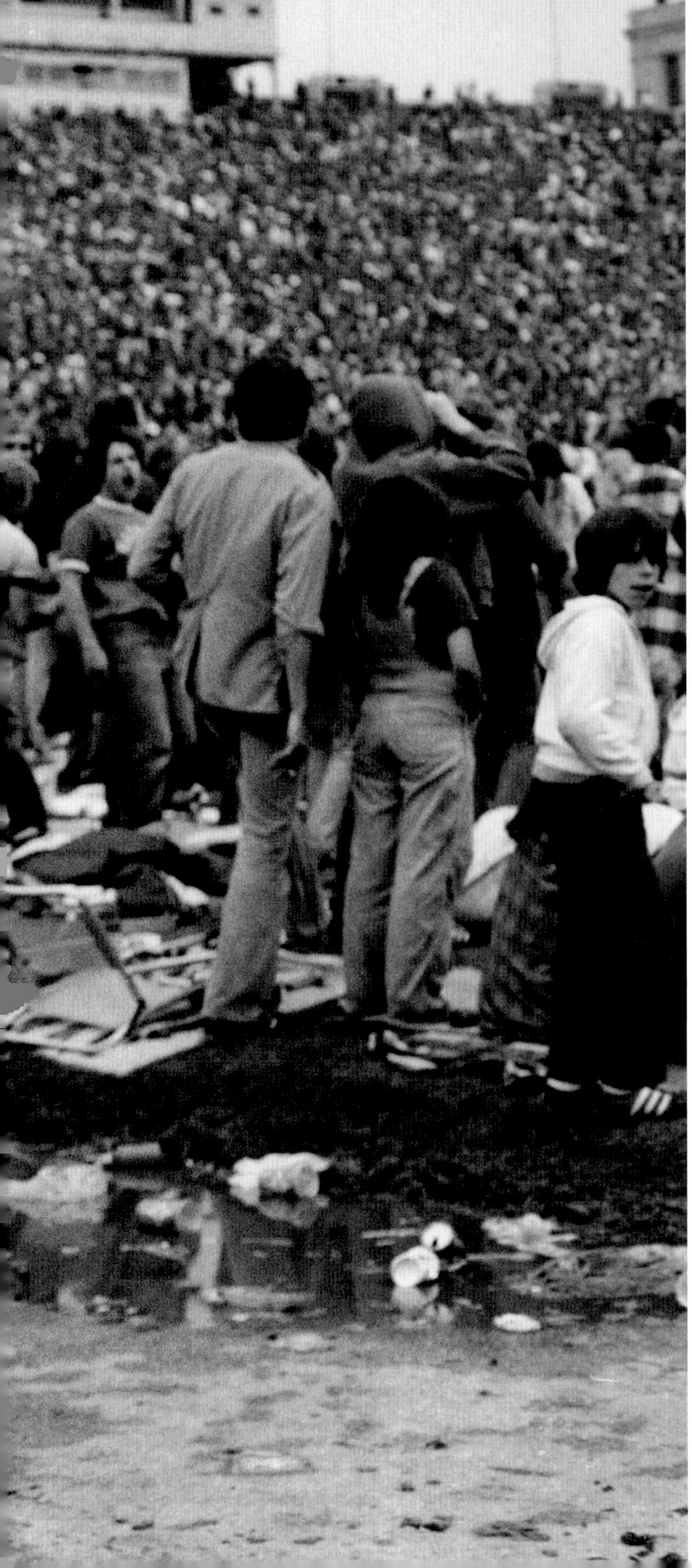

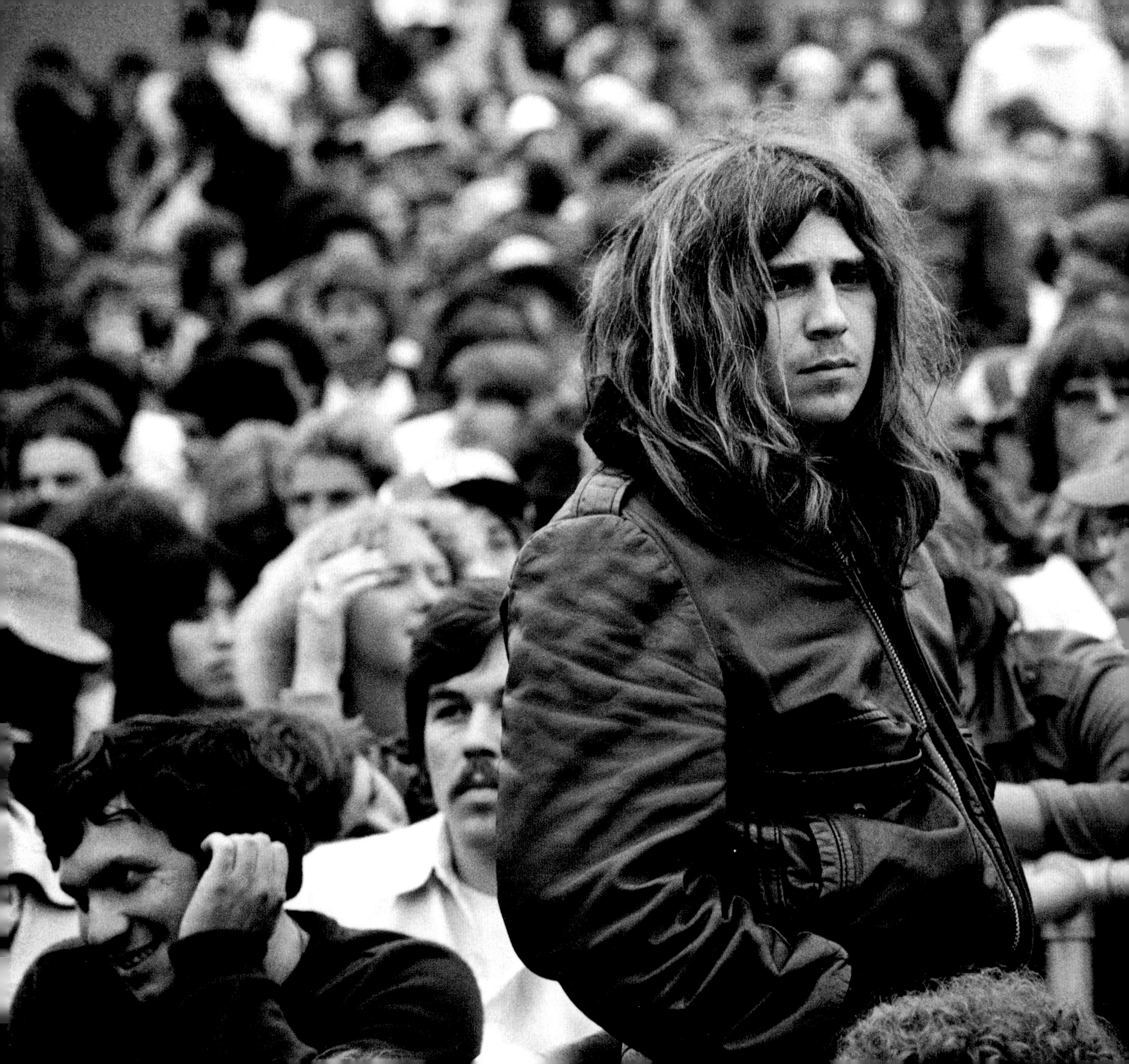

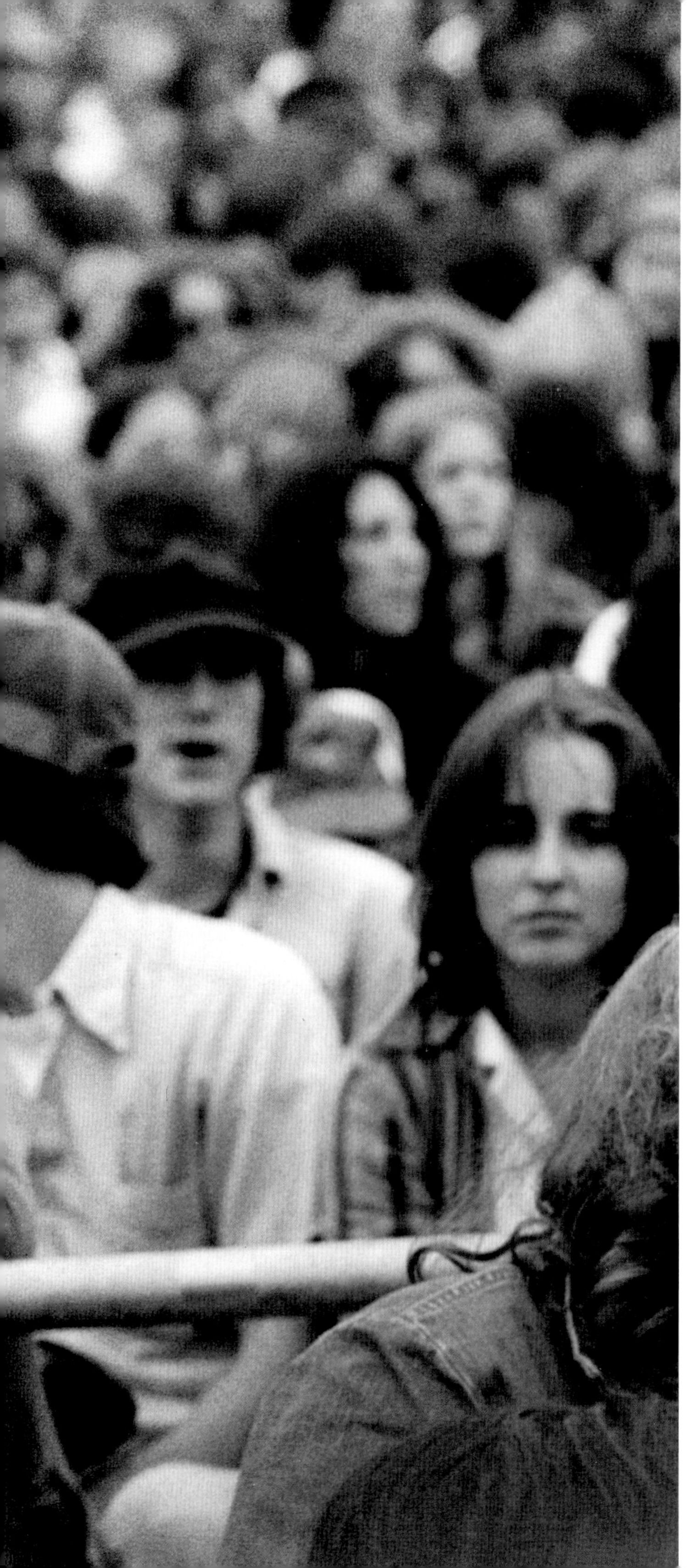

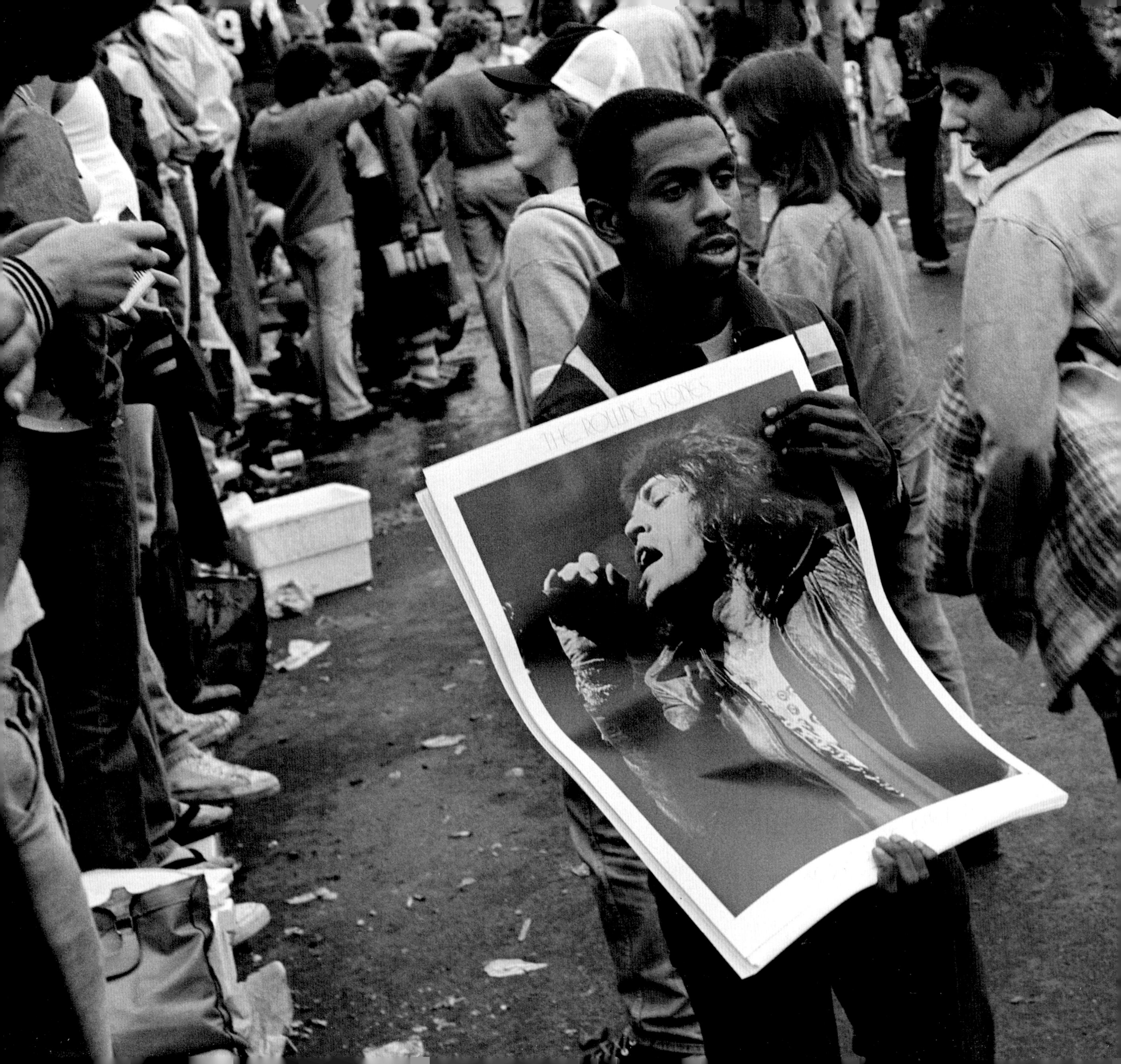
THE ROLLING STONES

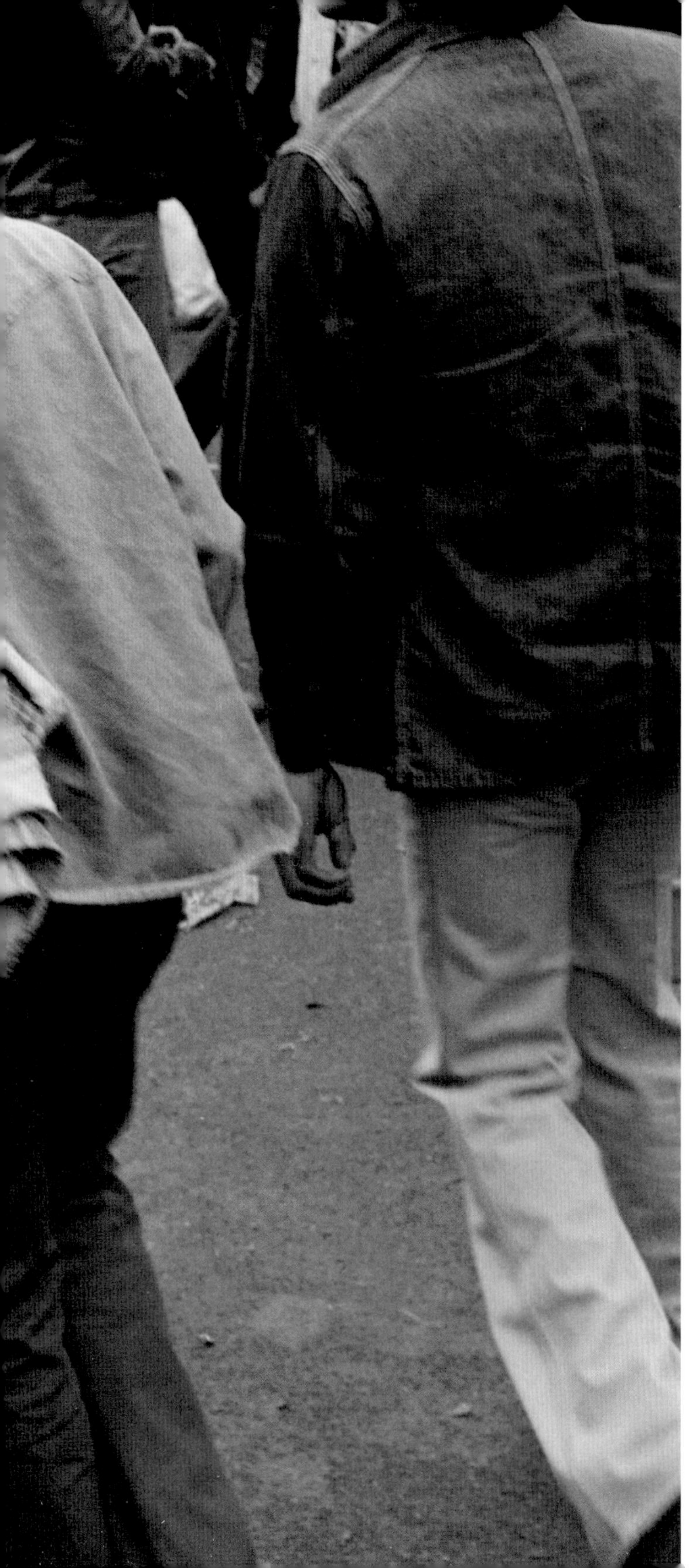

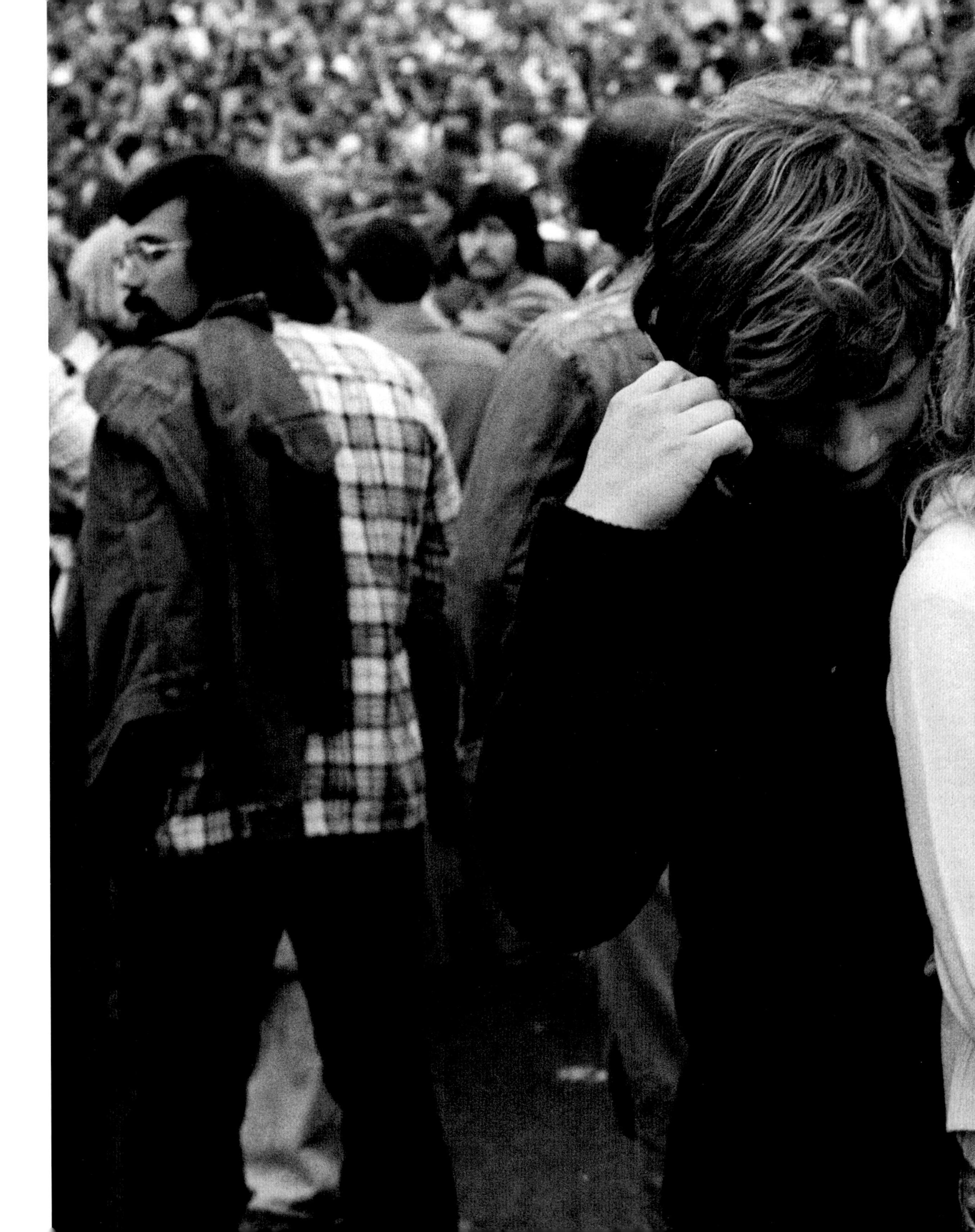

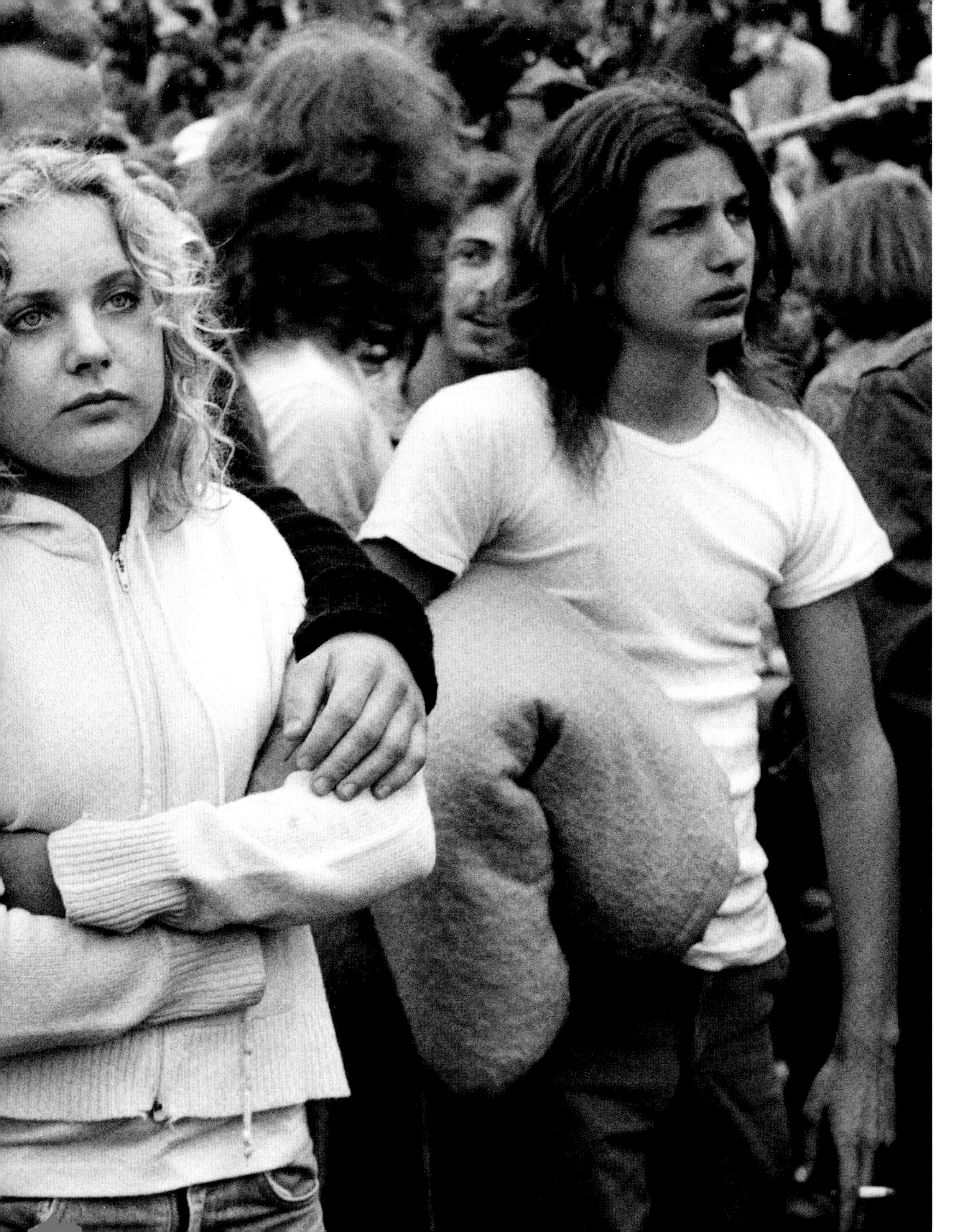

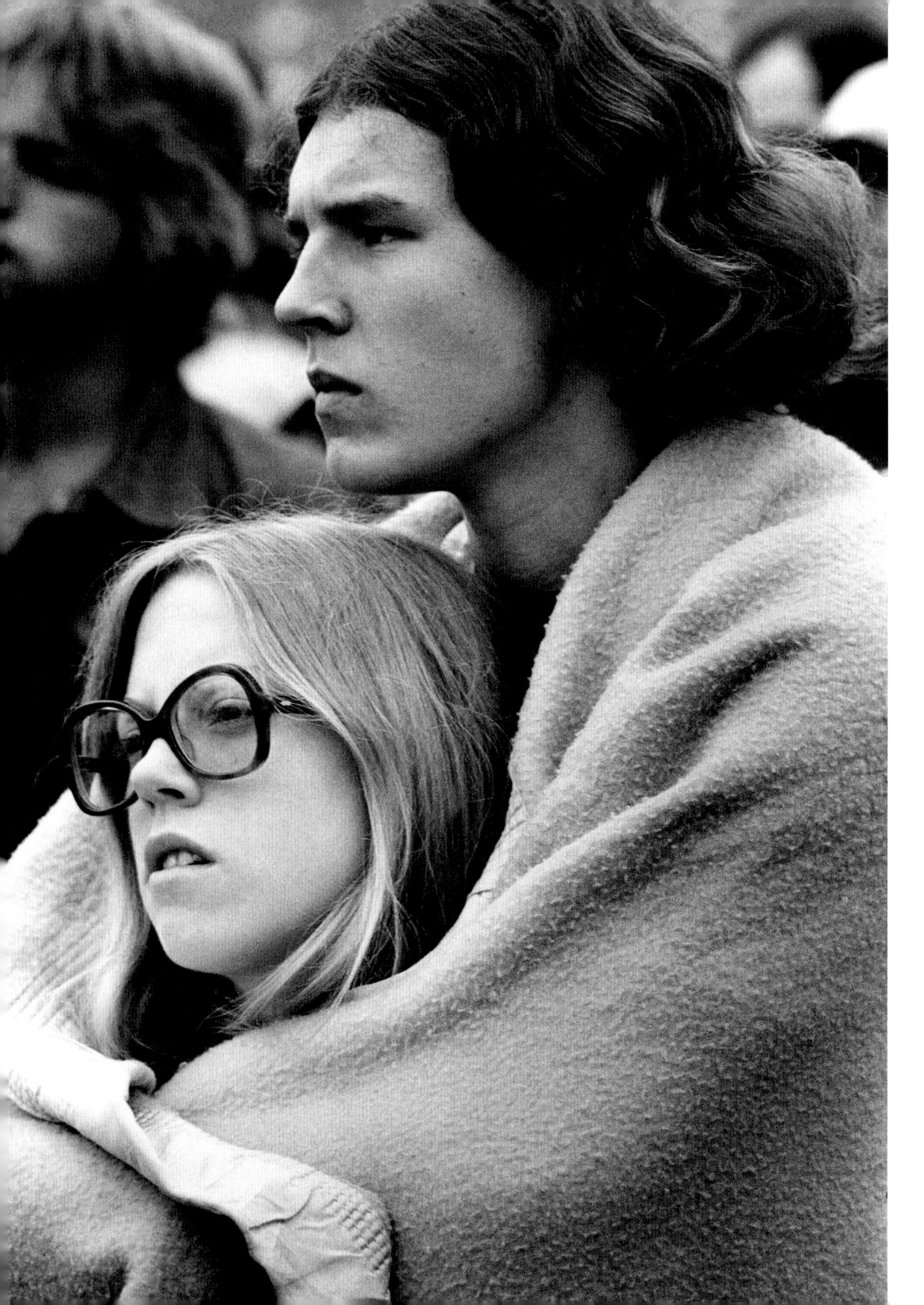

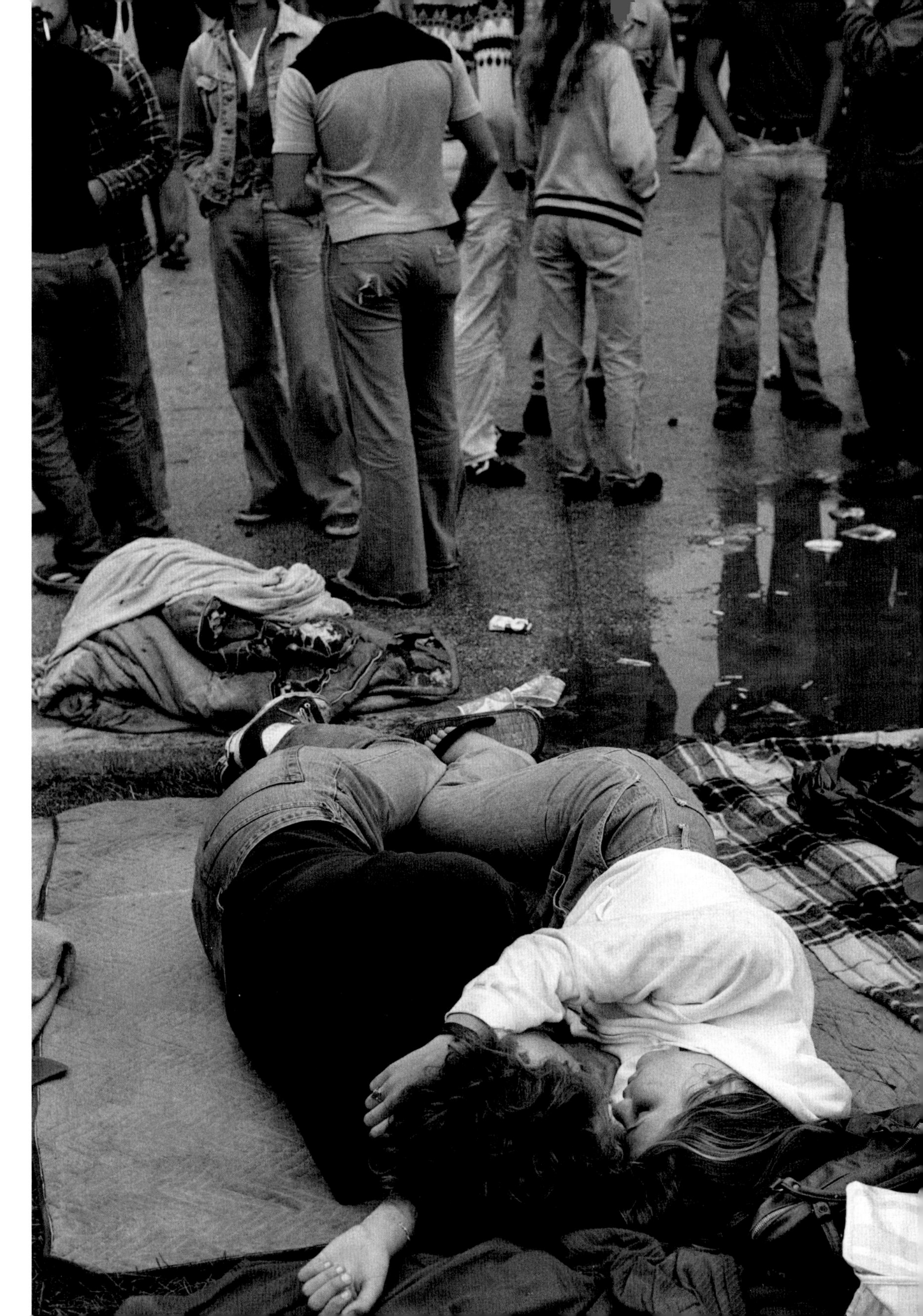

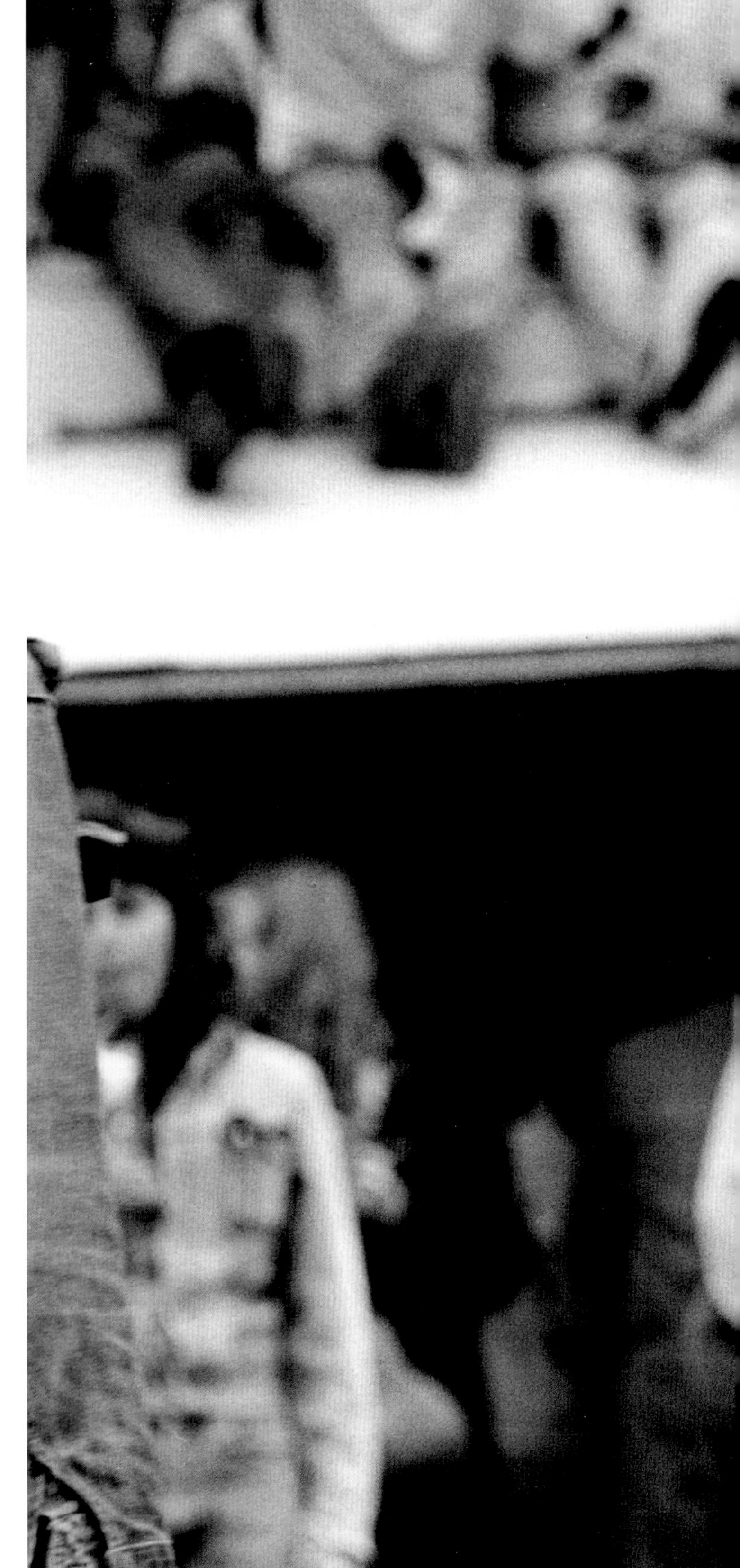

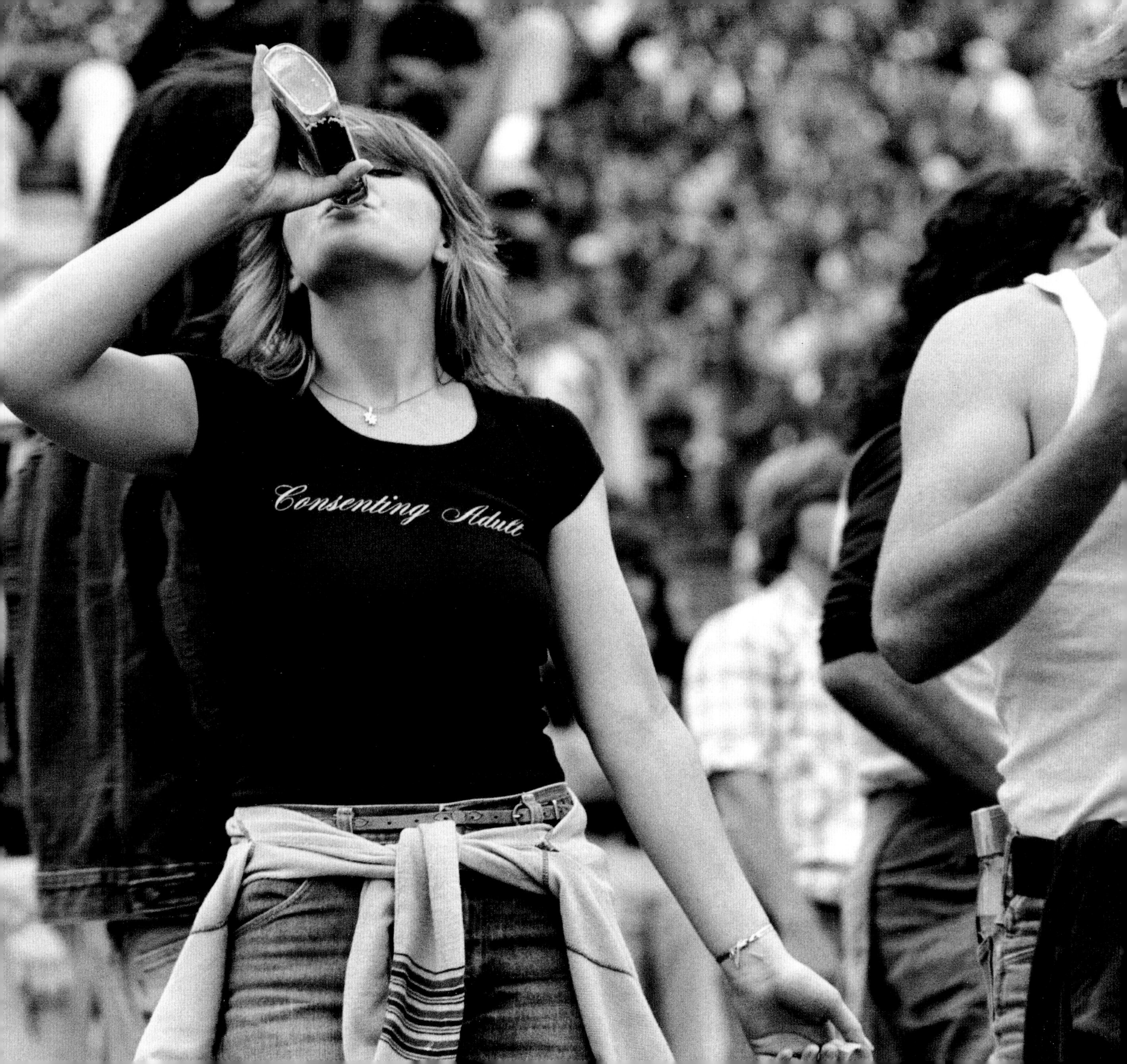

Consenting Adult

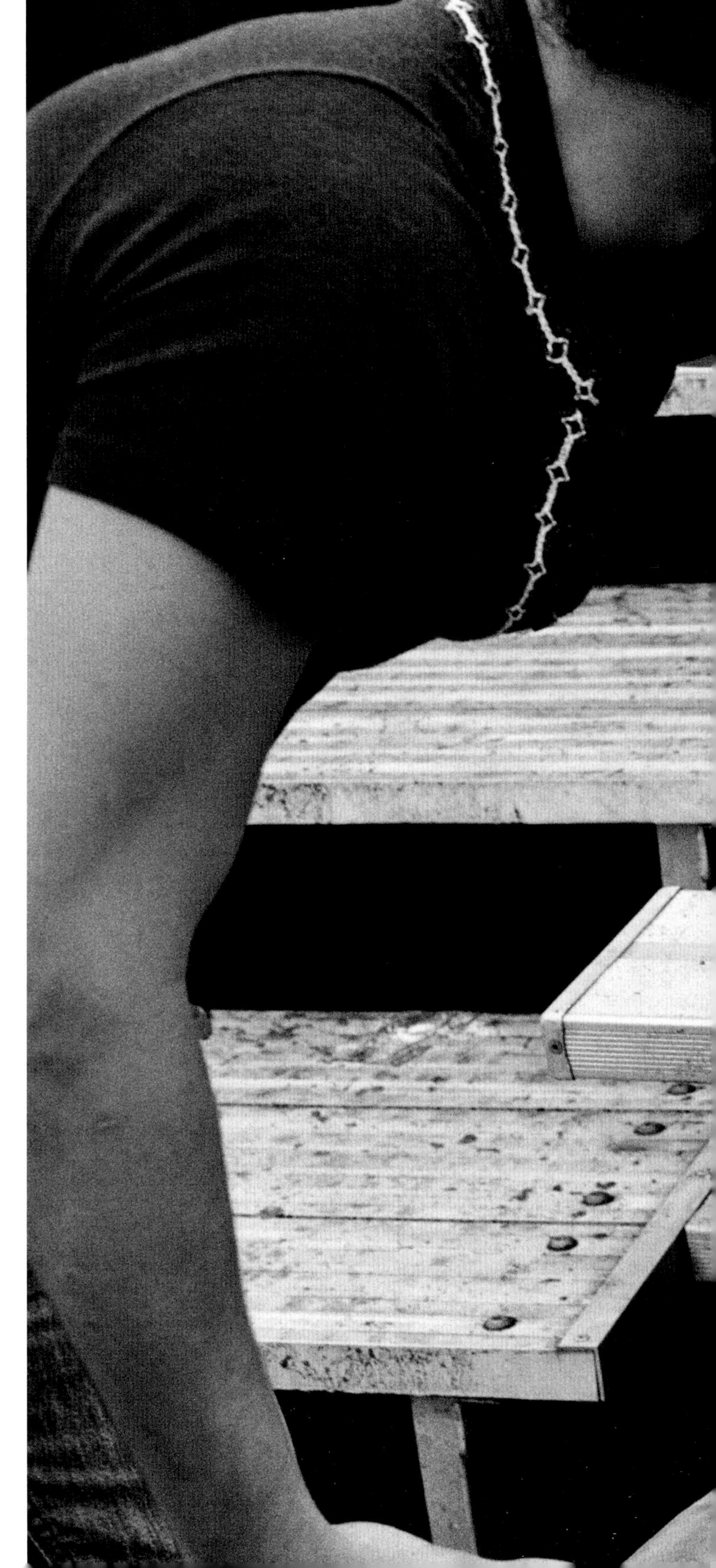

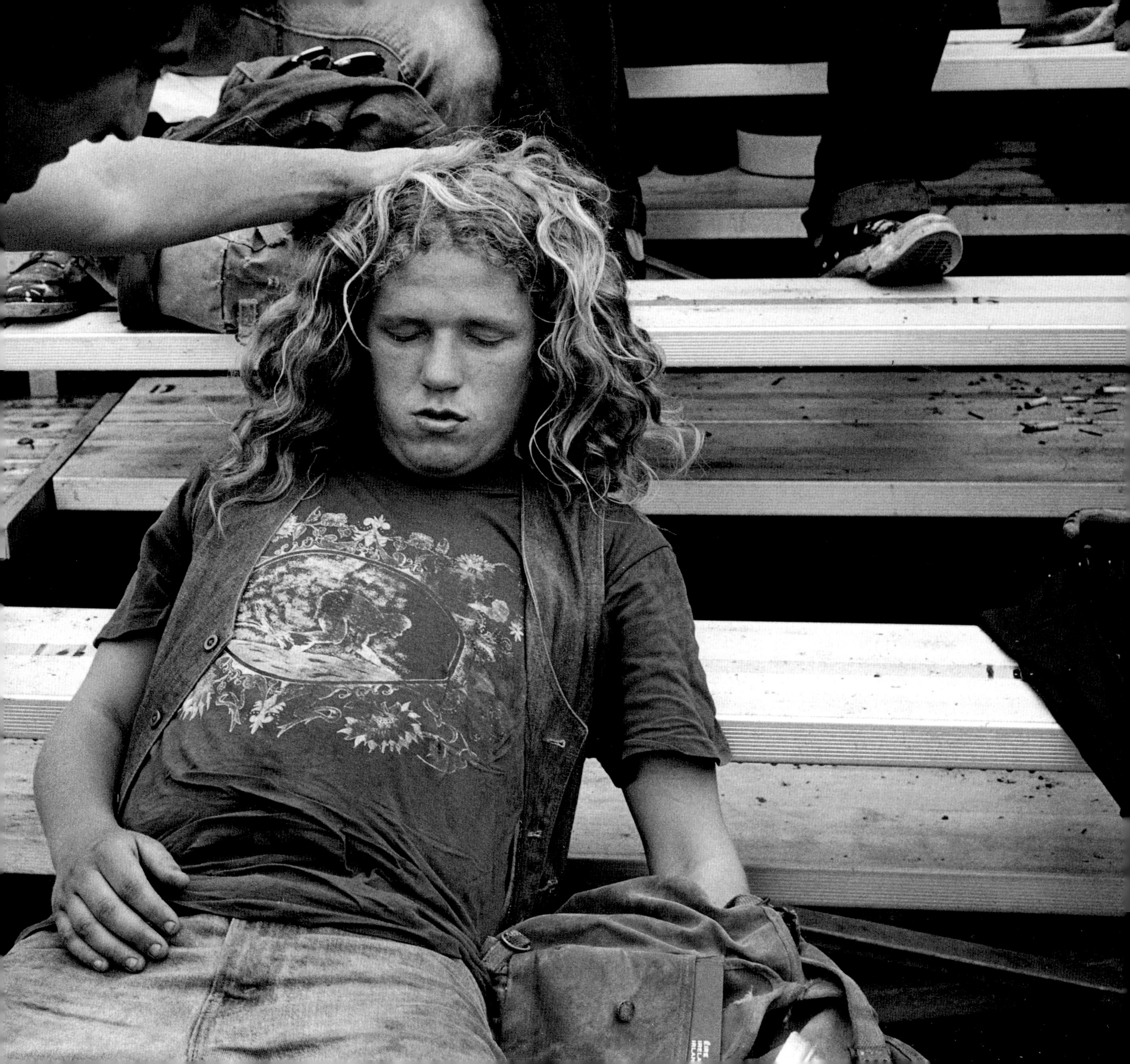

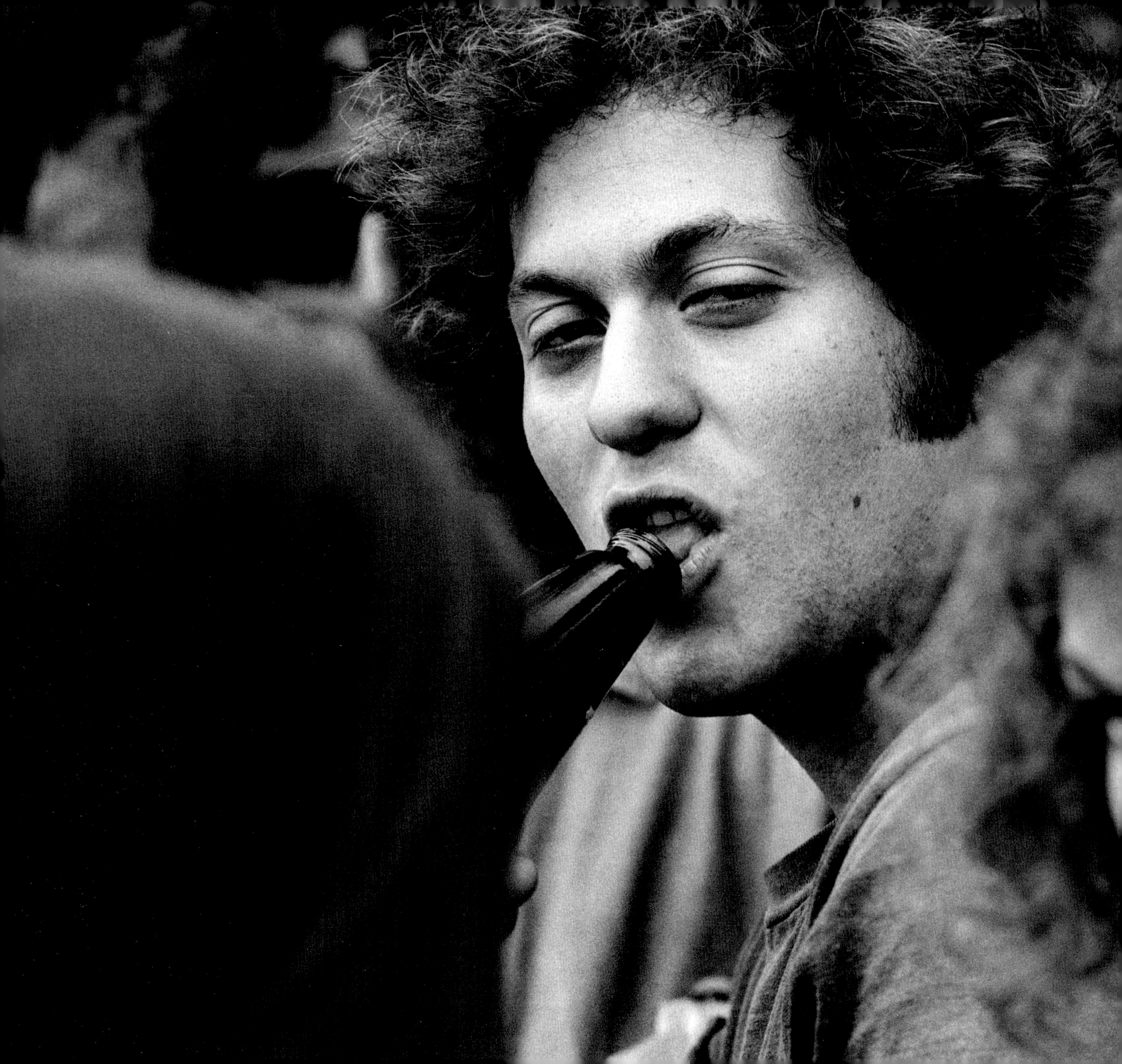

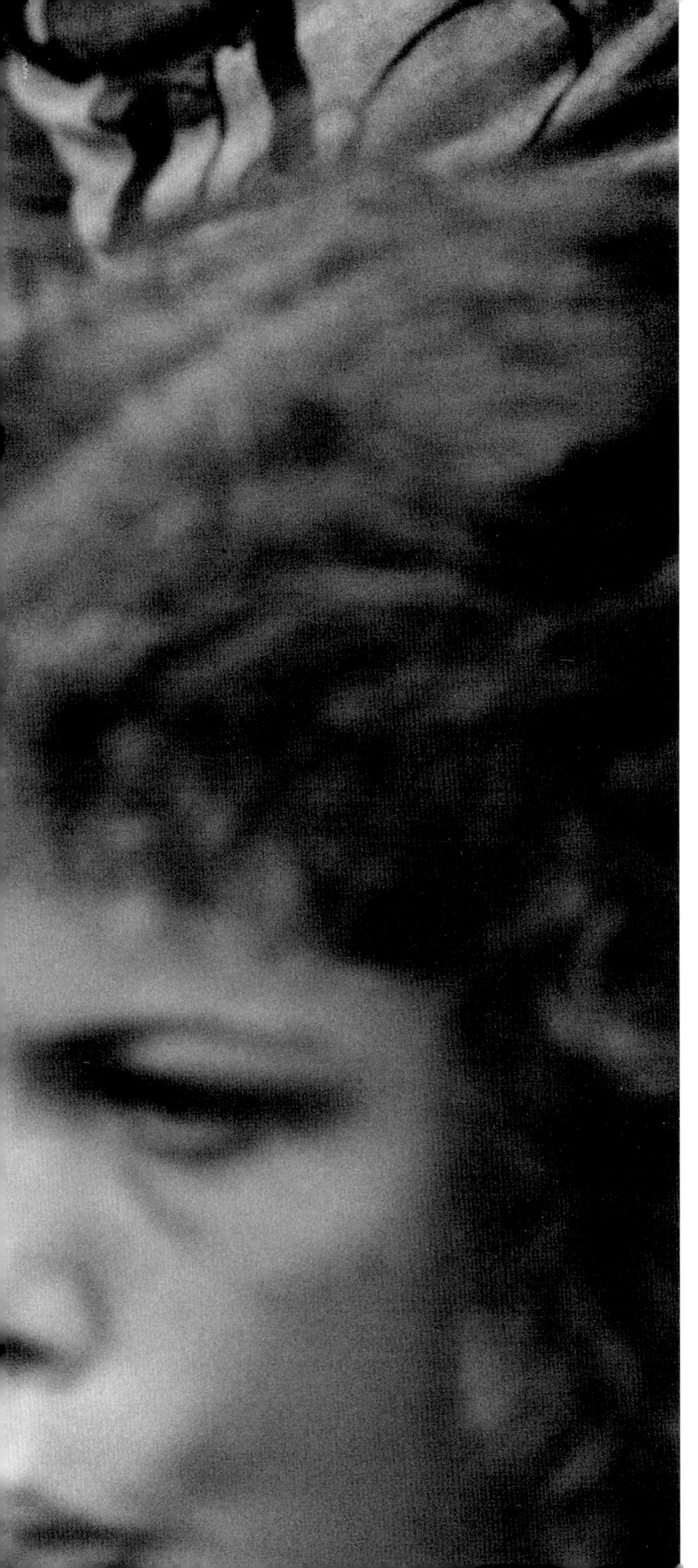

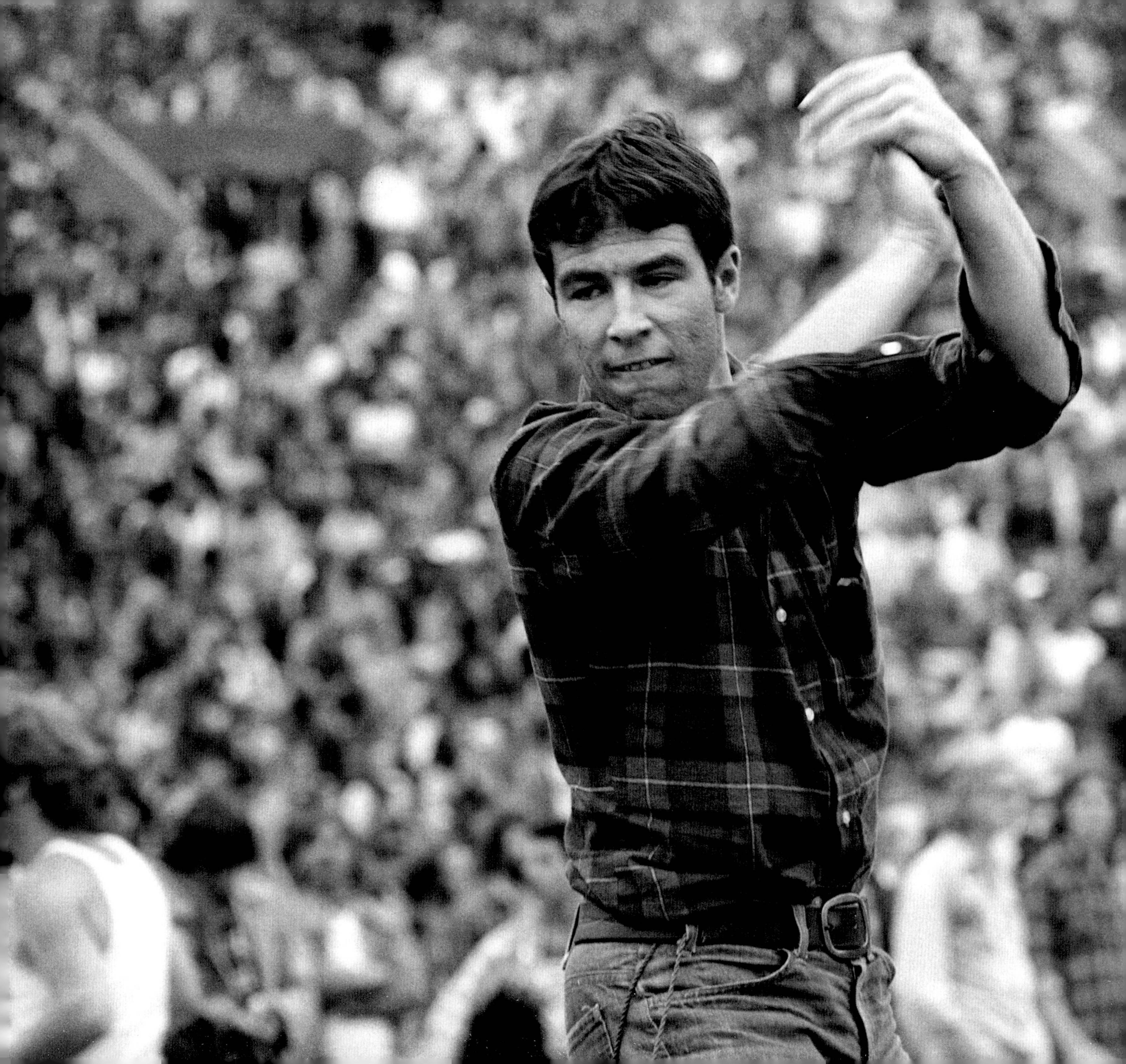

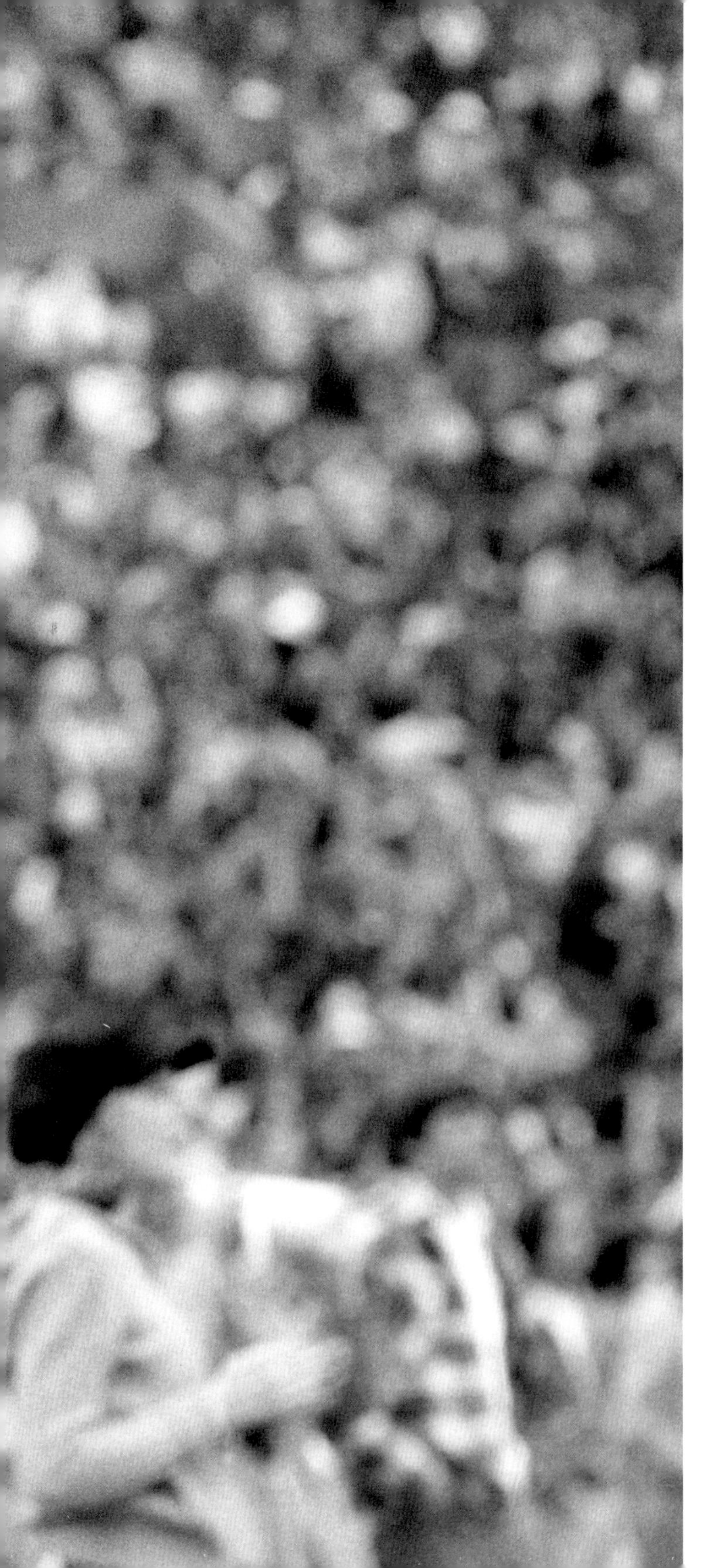

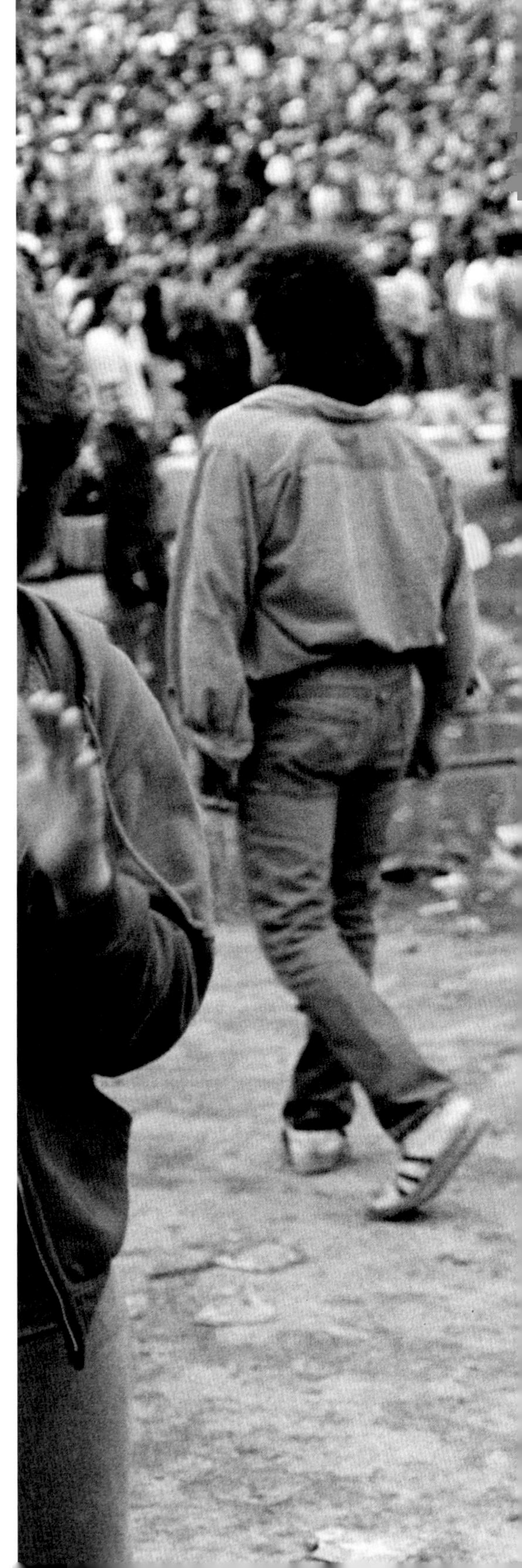

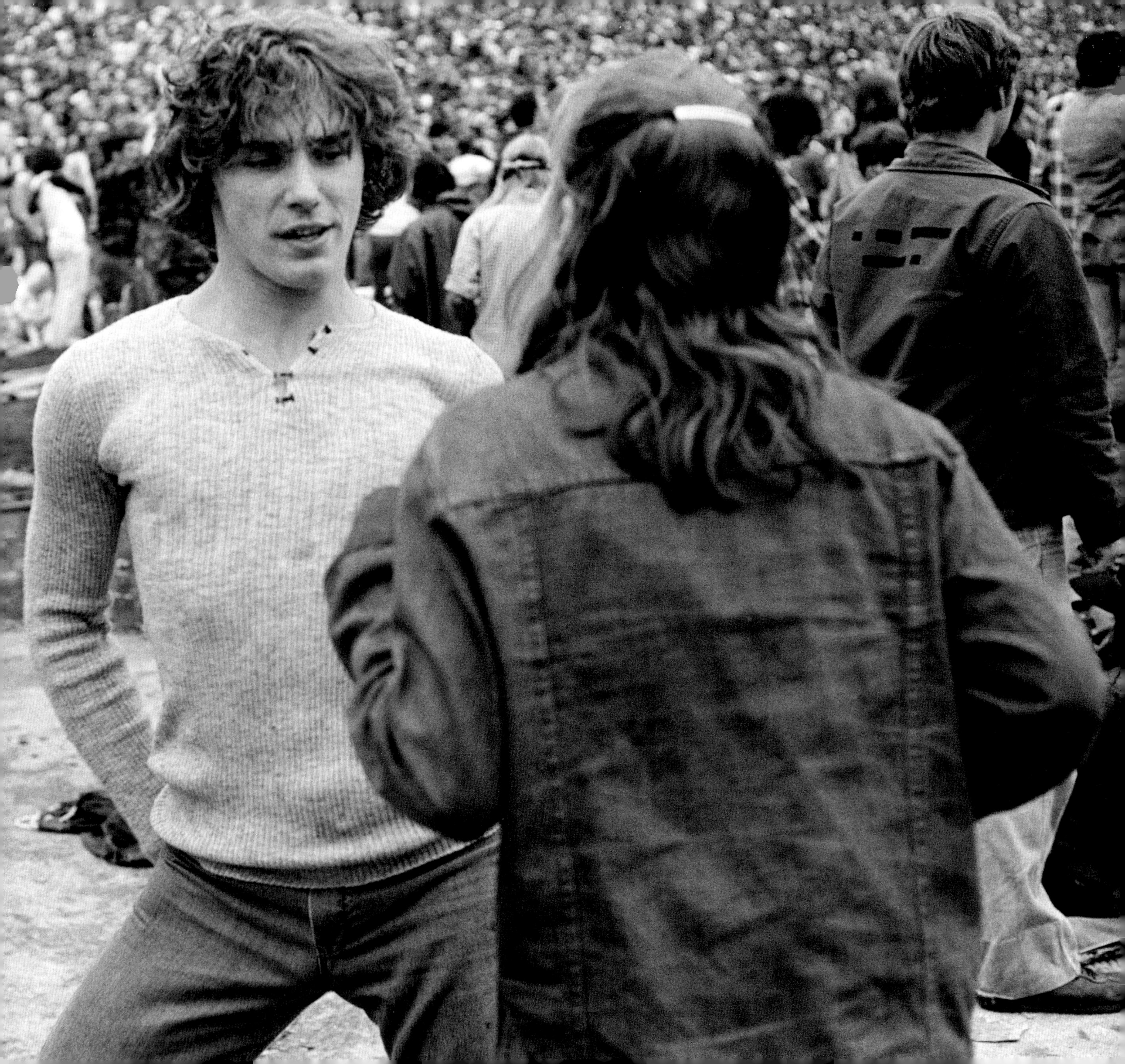

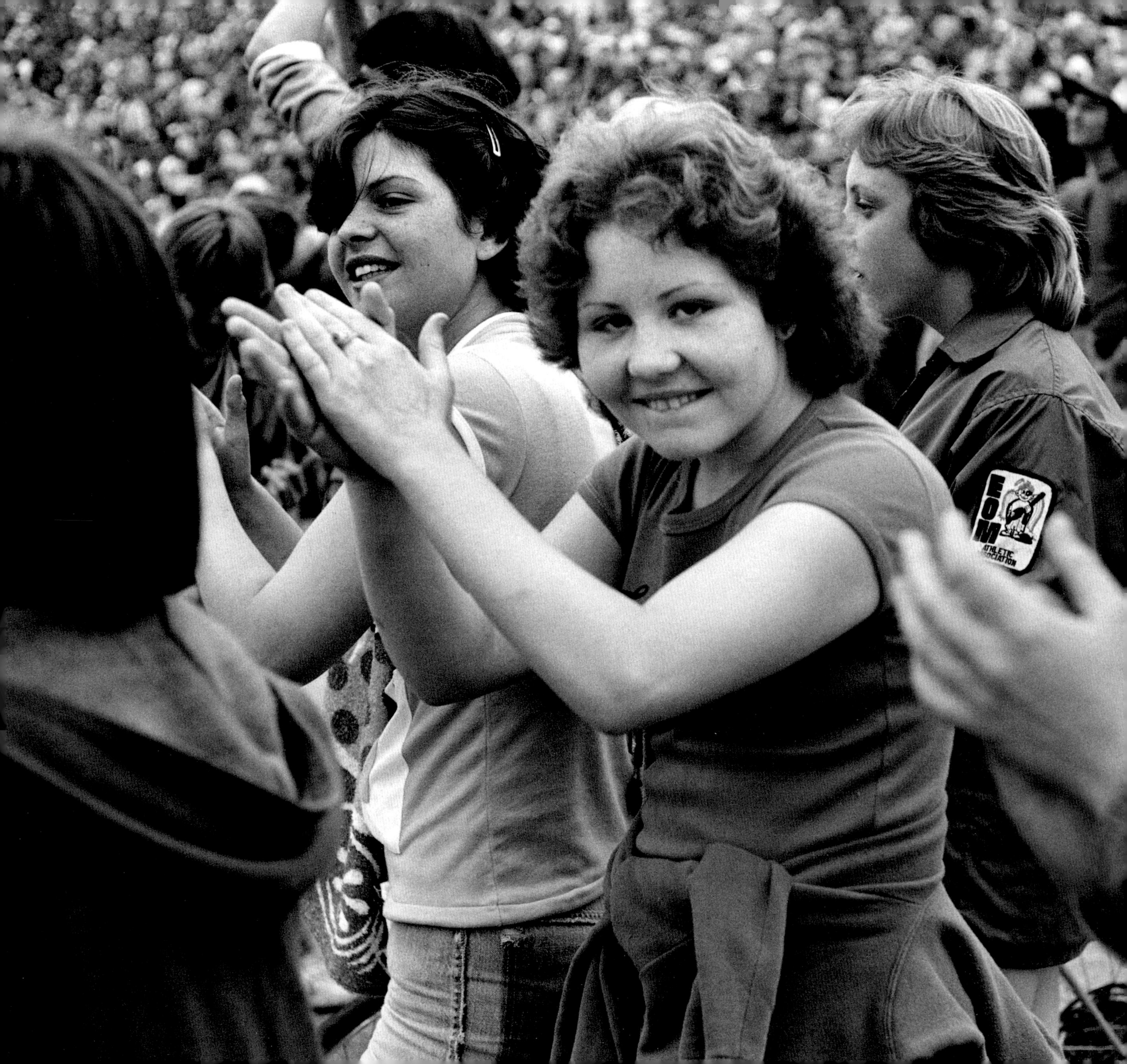

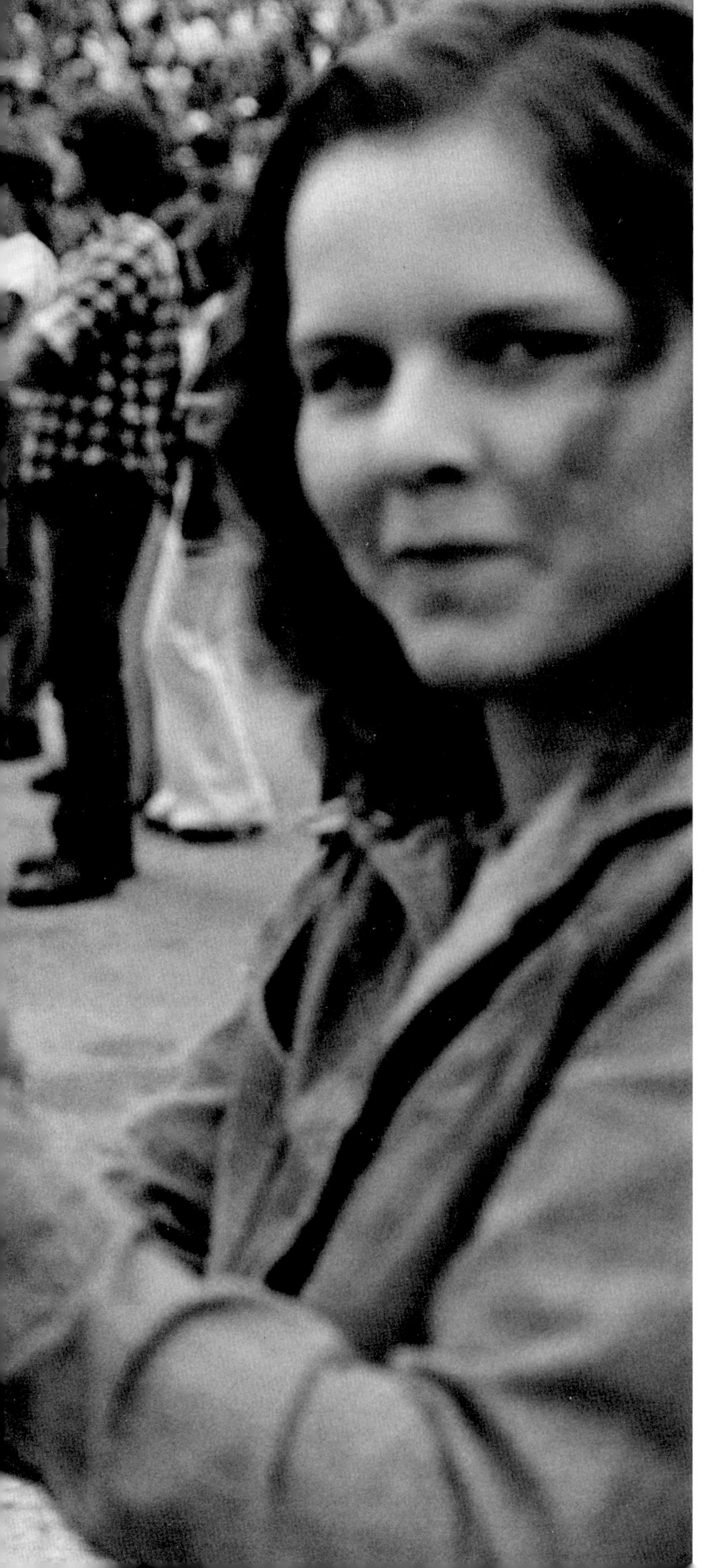

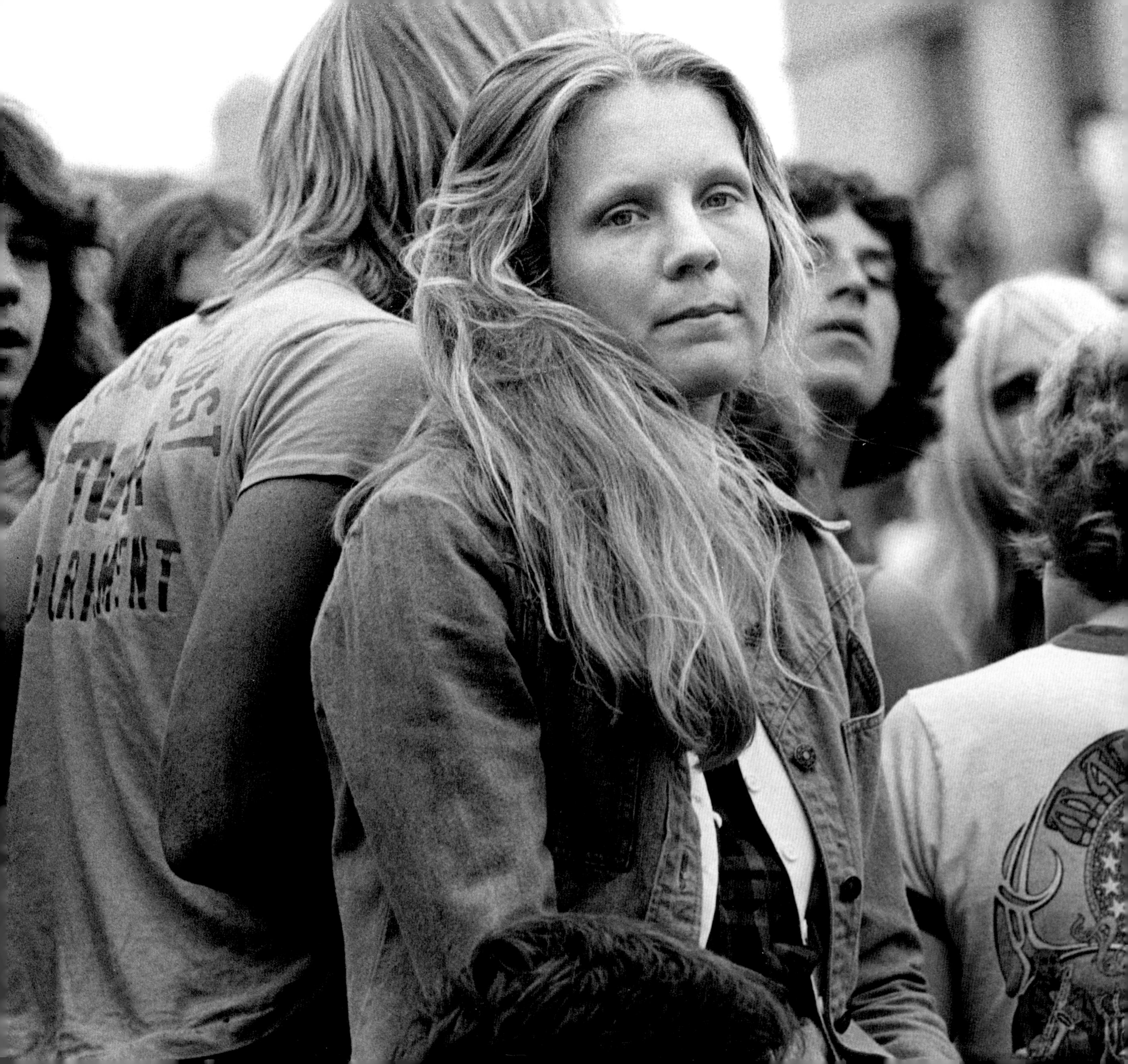

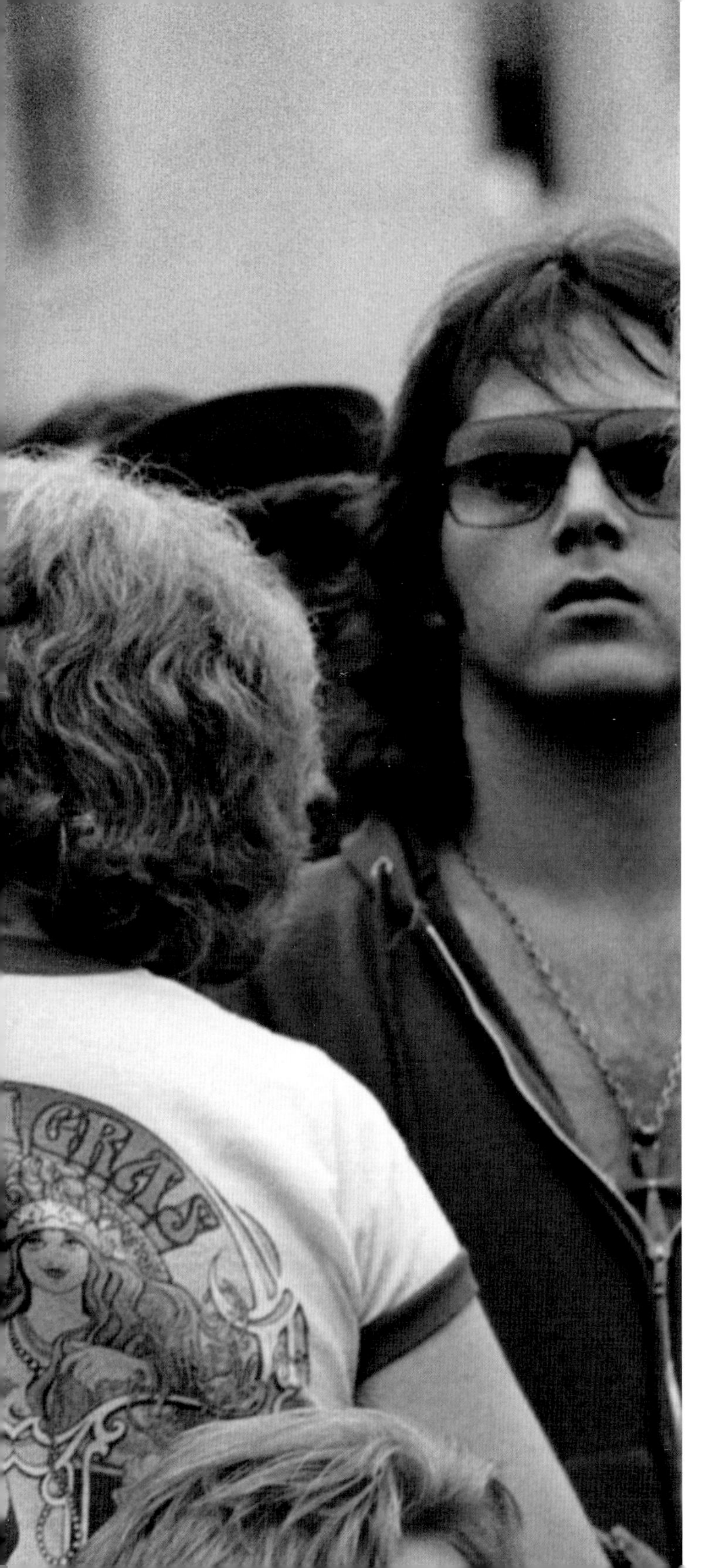

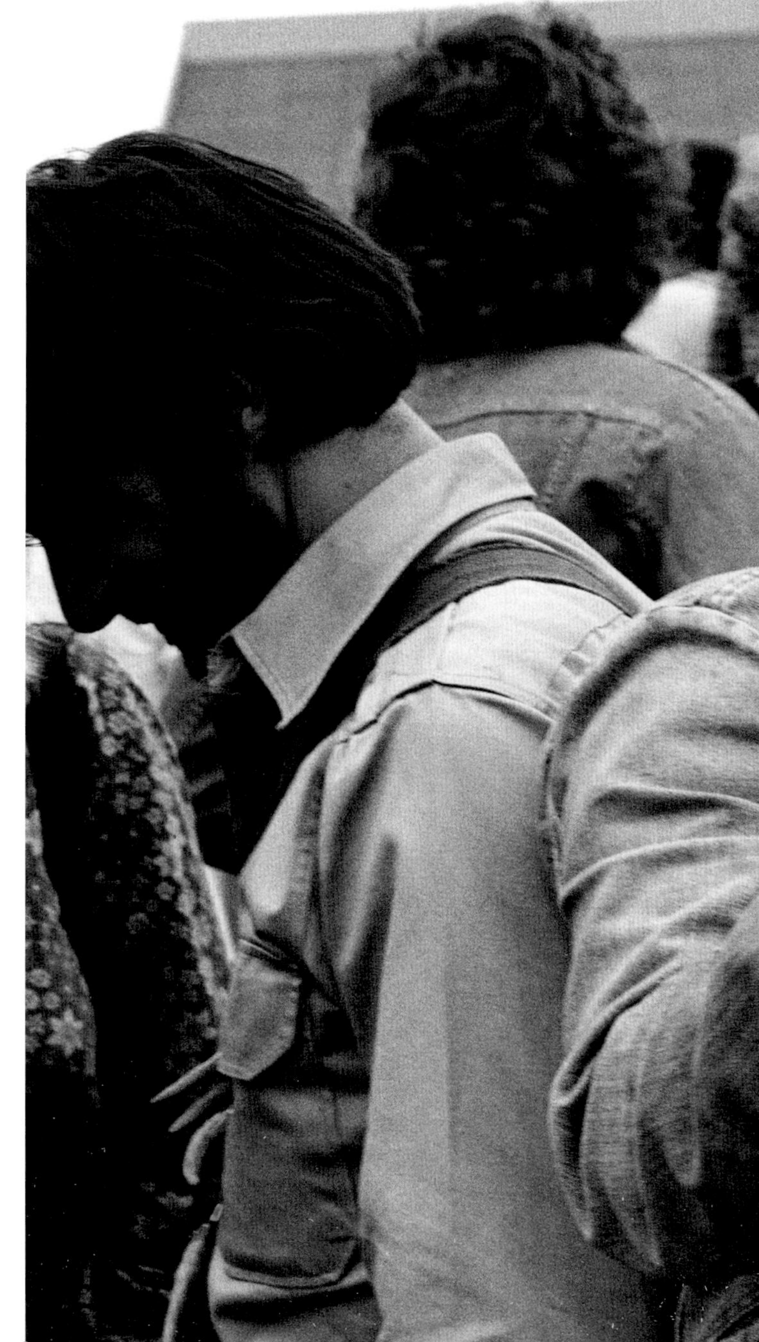

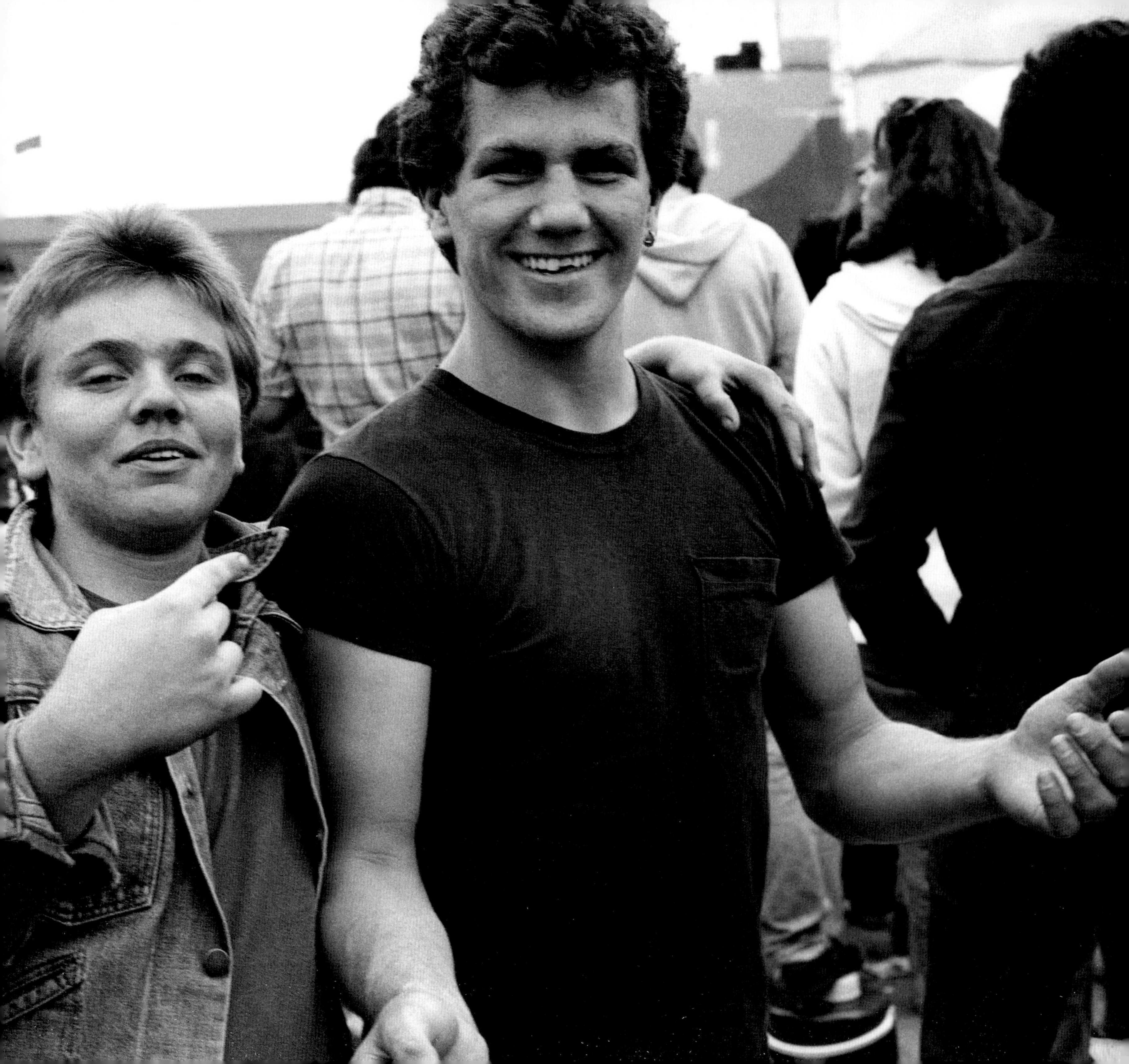

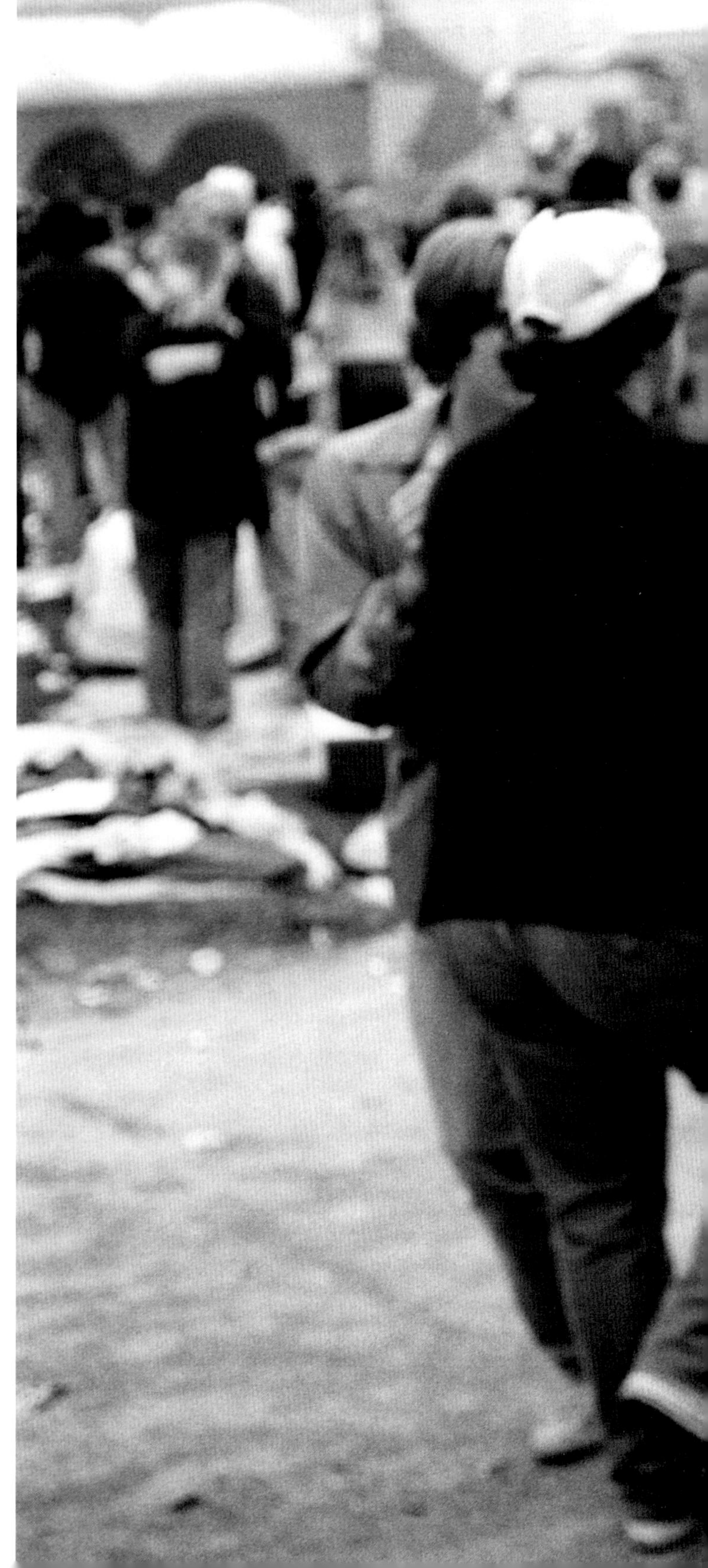

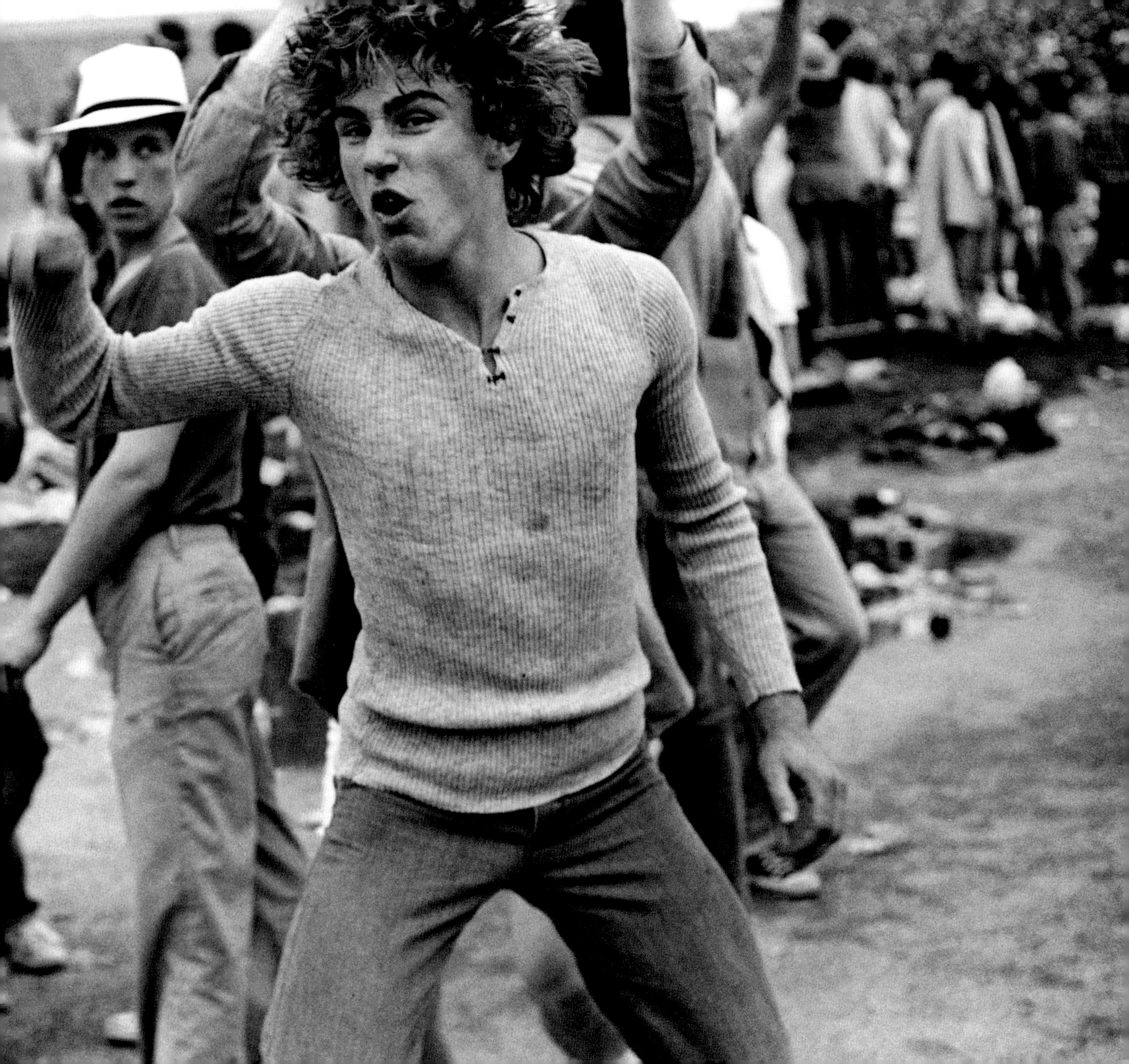

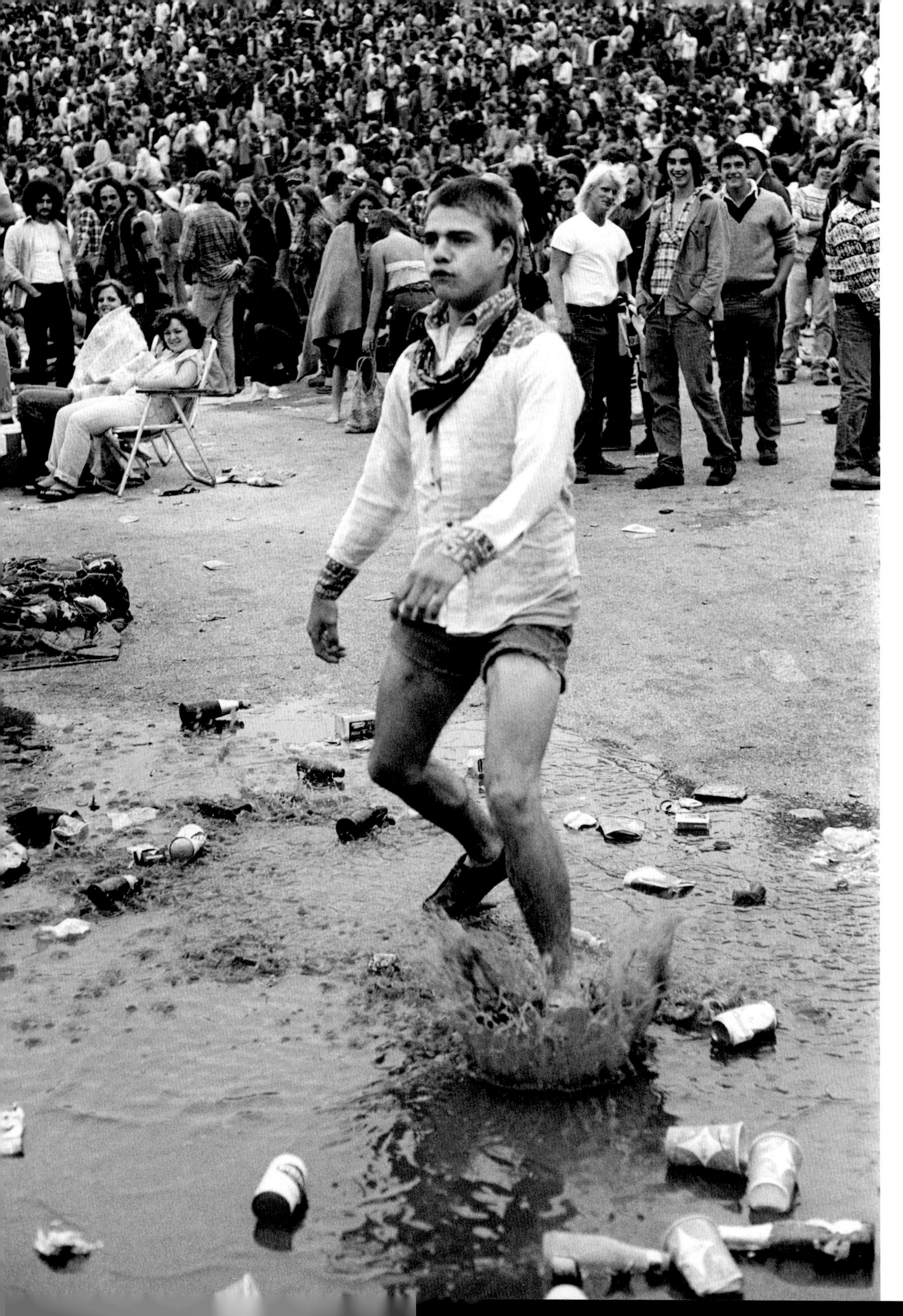

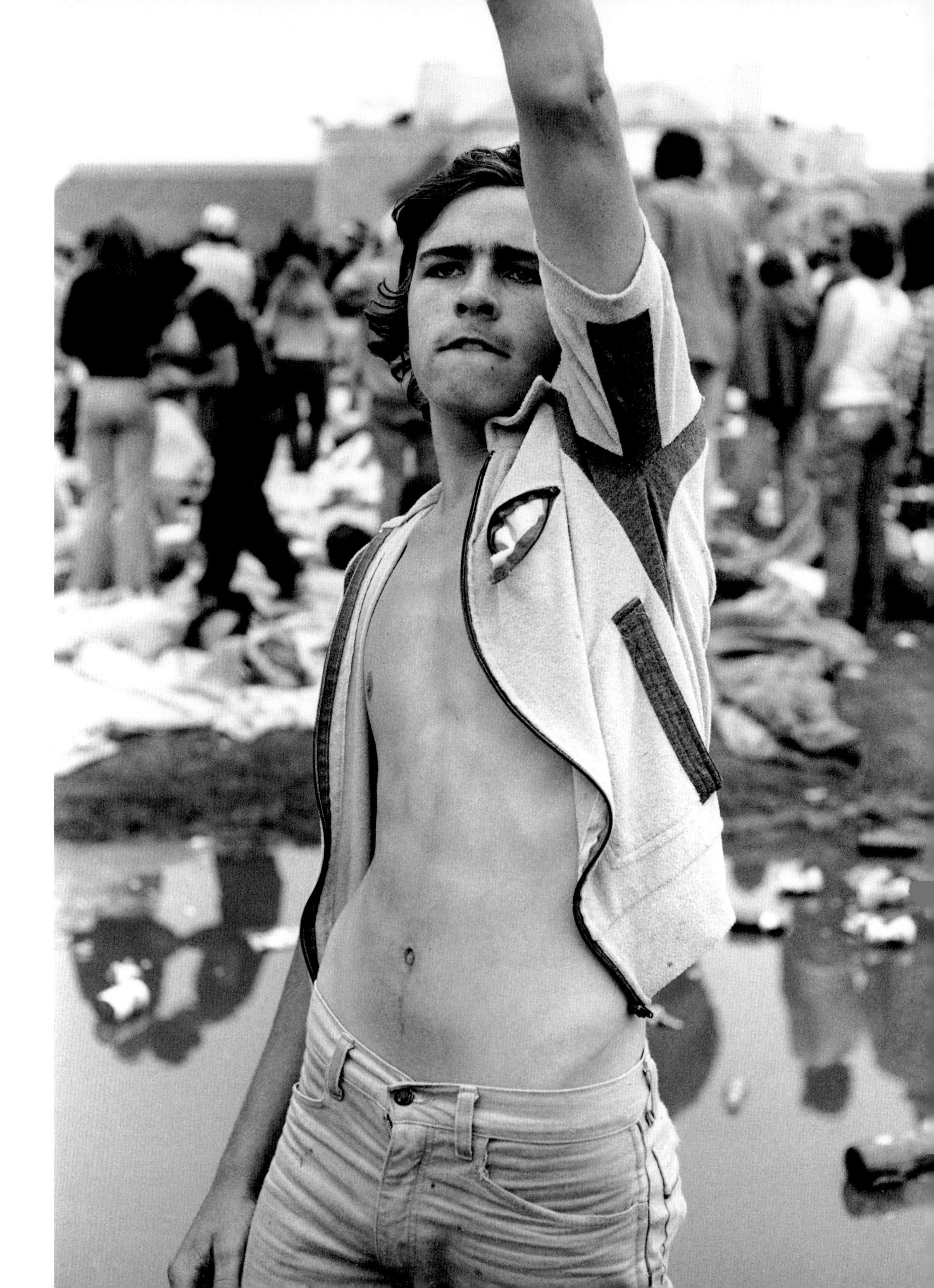

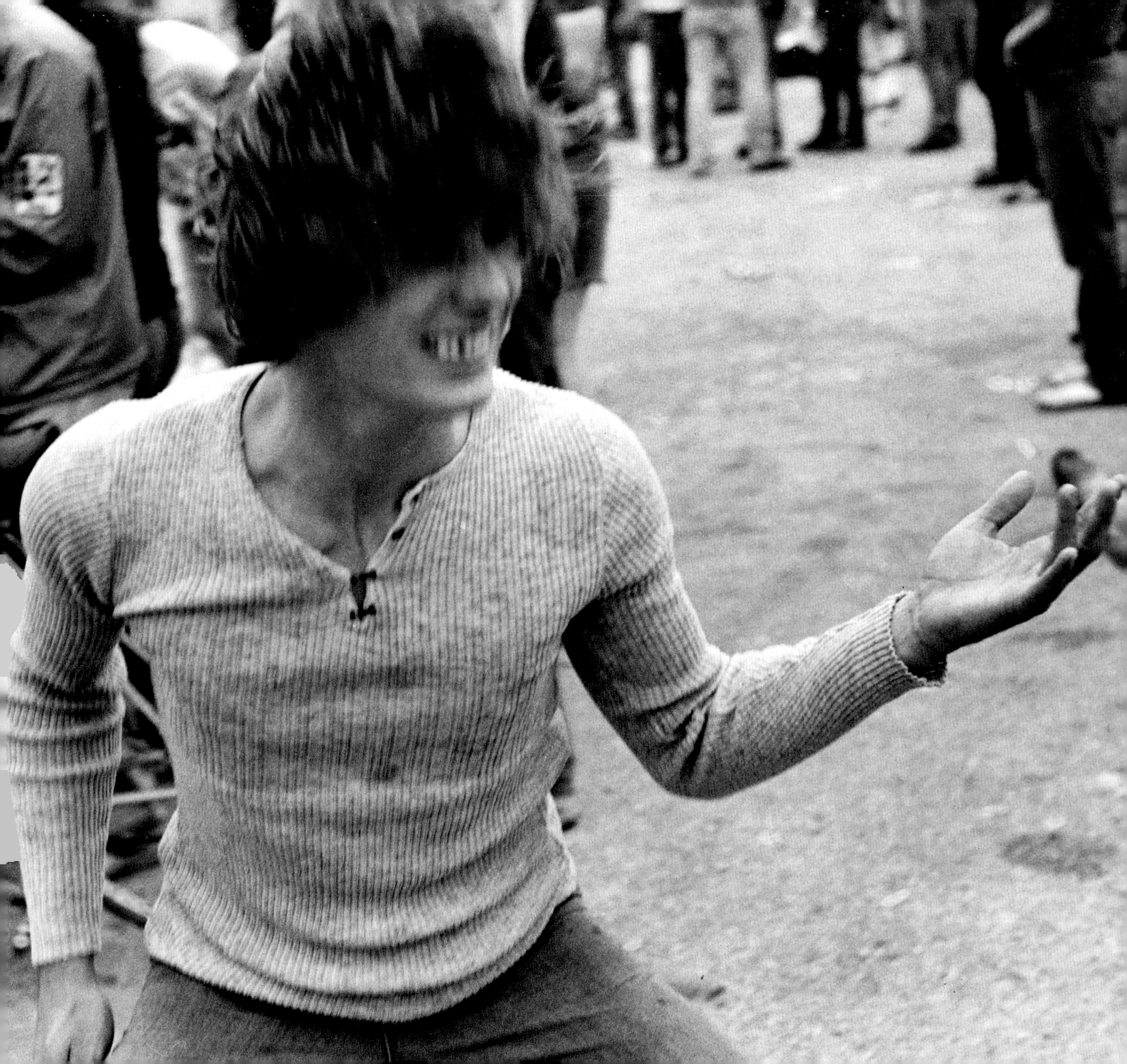

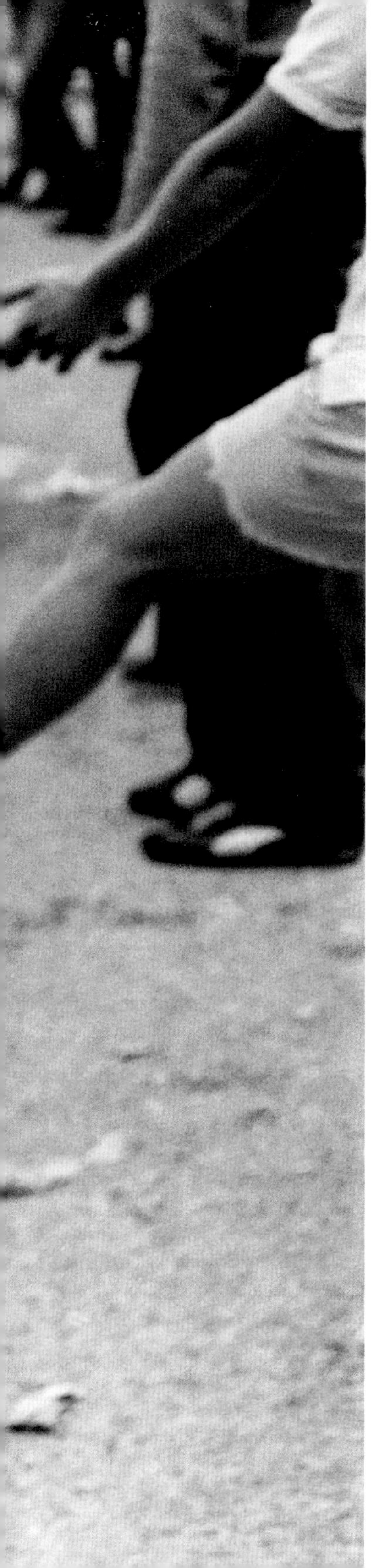

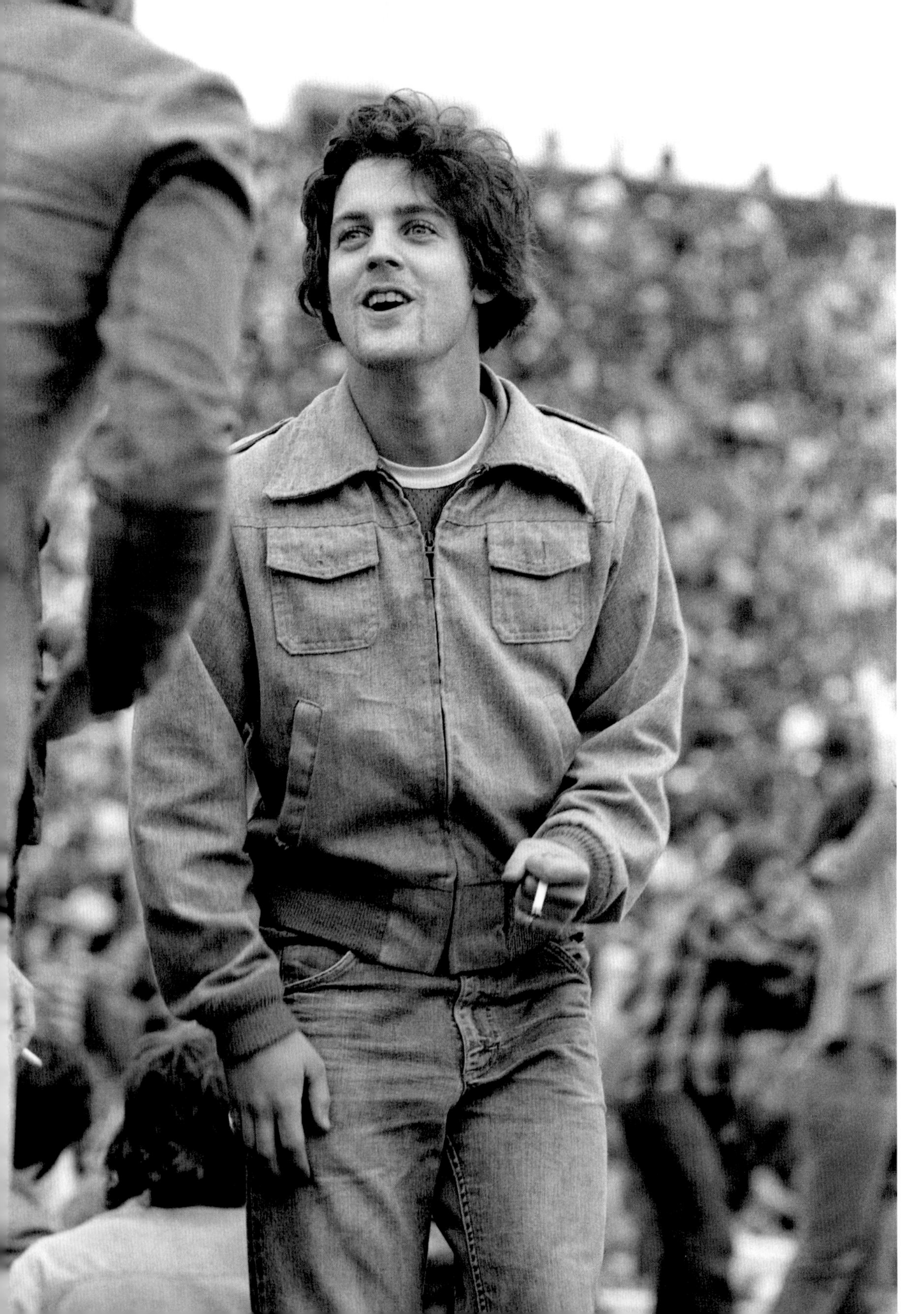

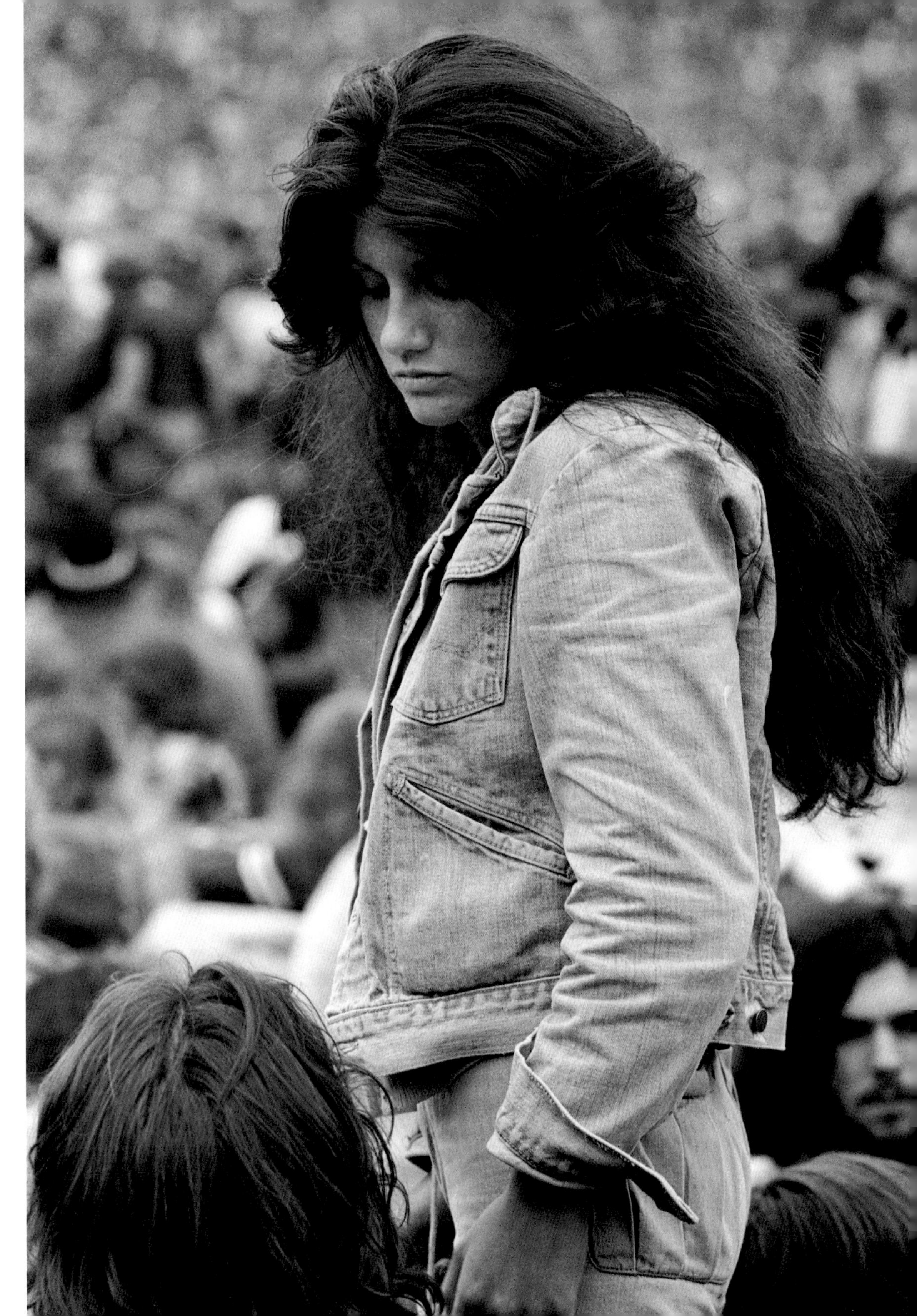

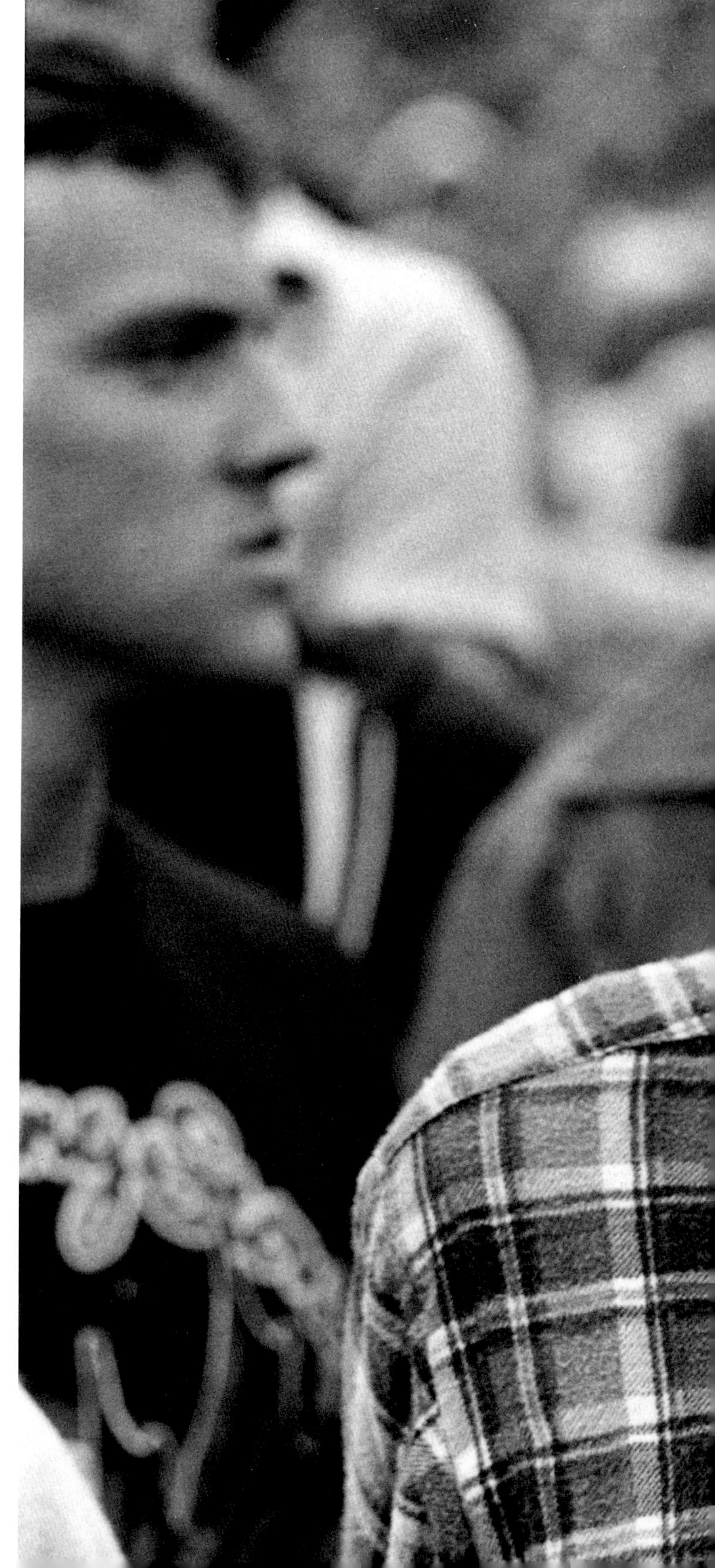

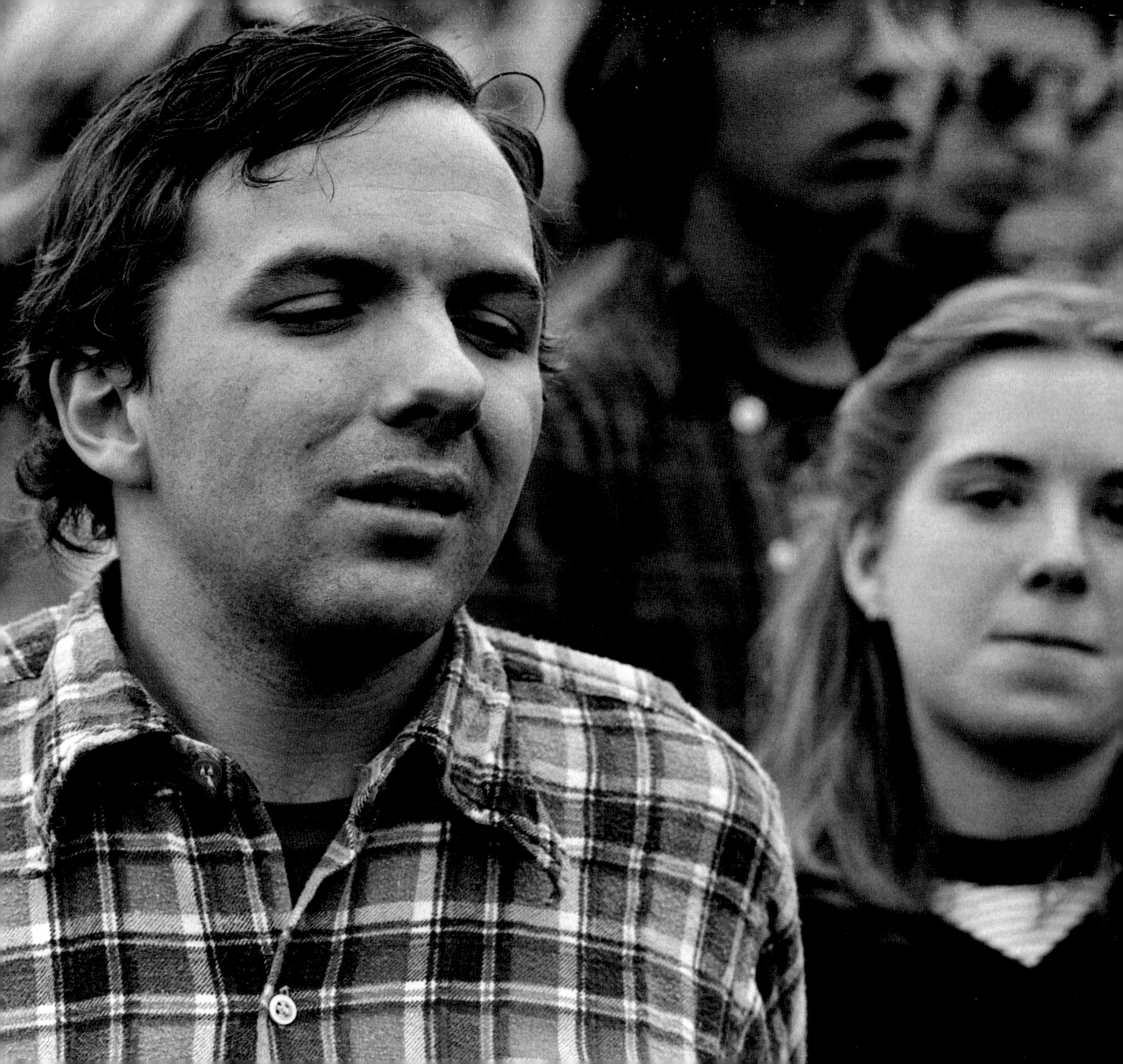

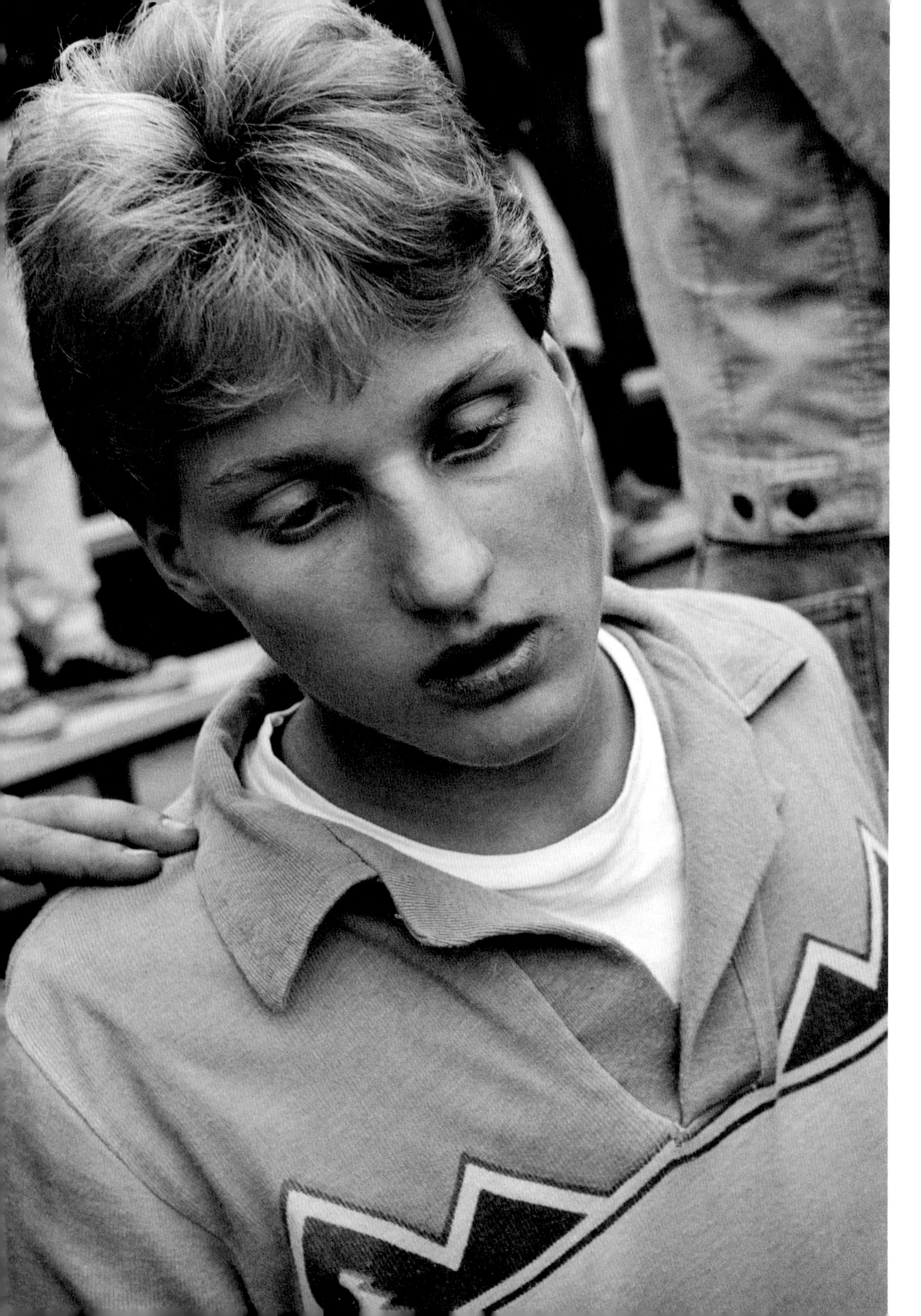

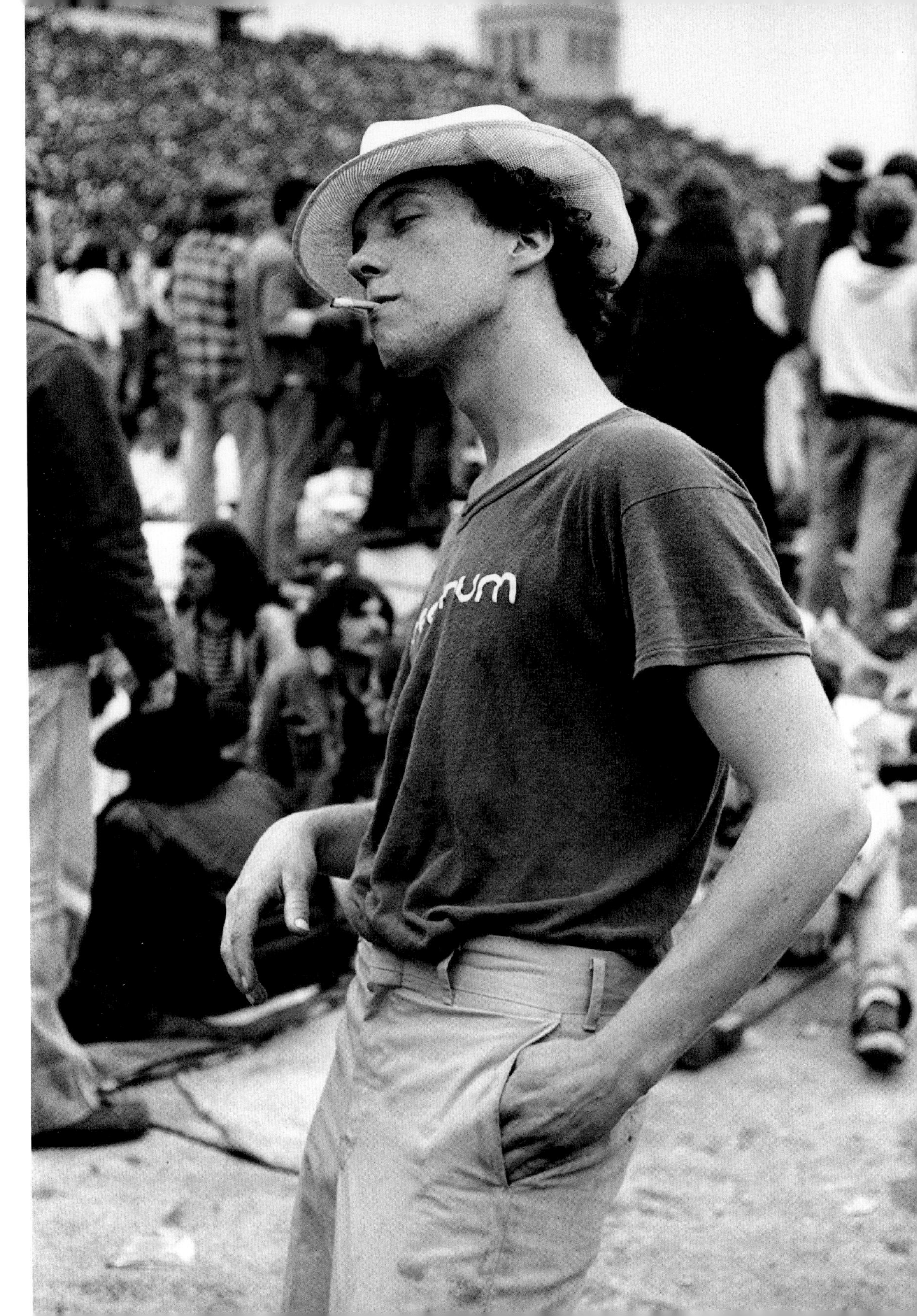

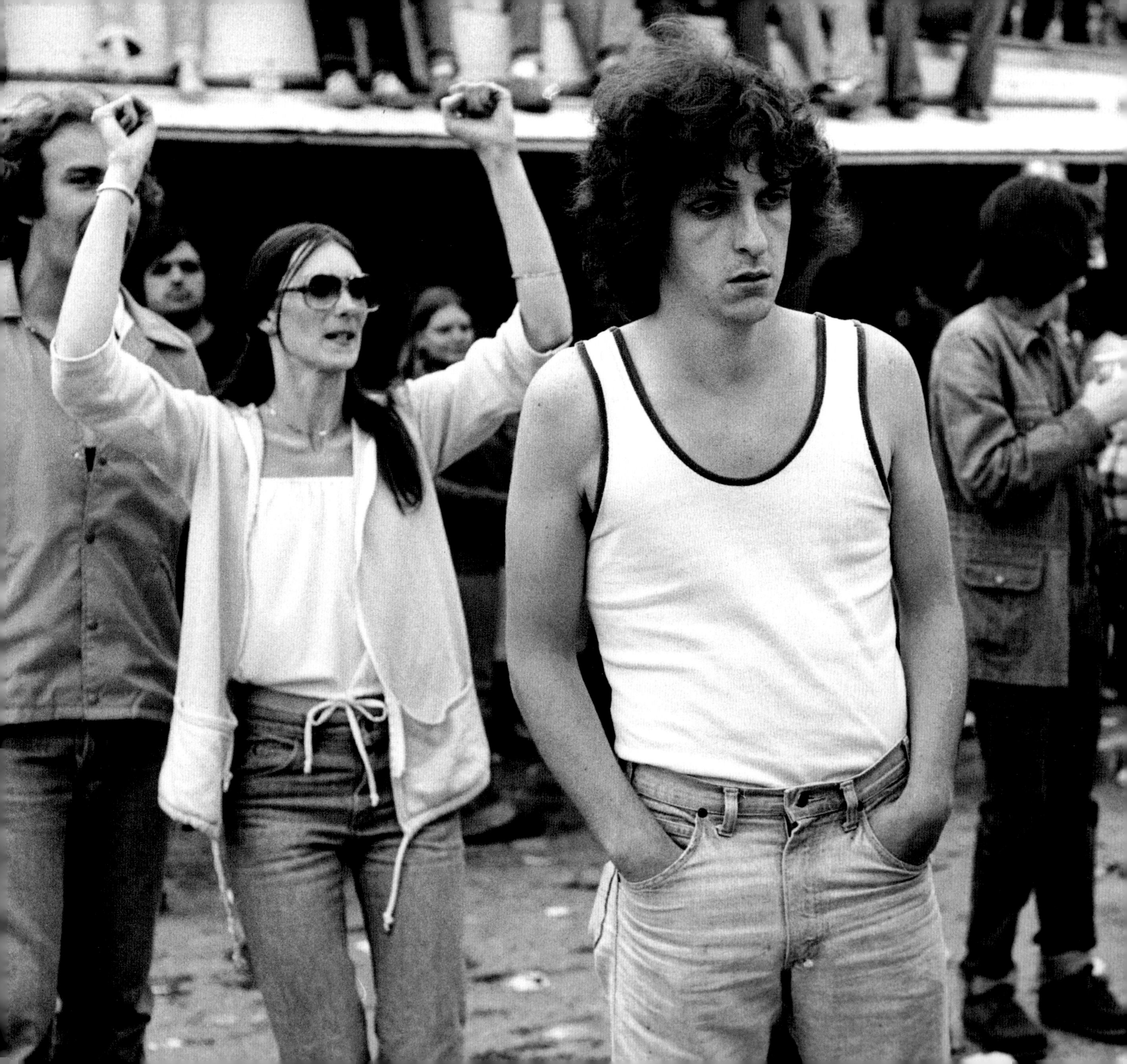

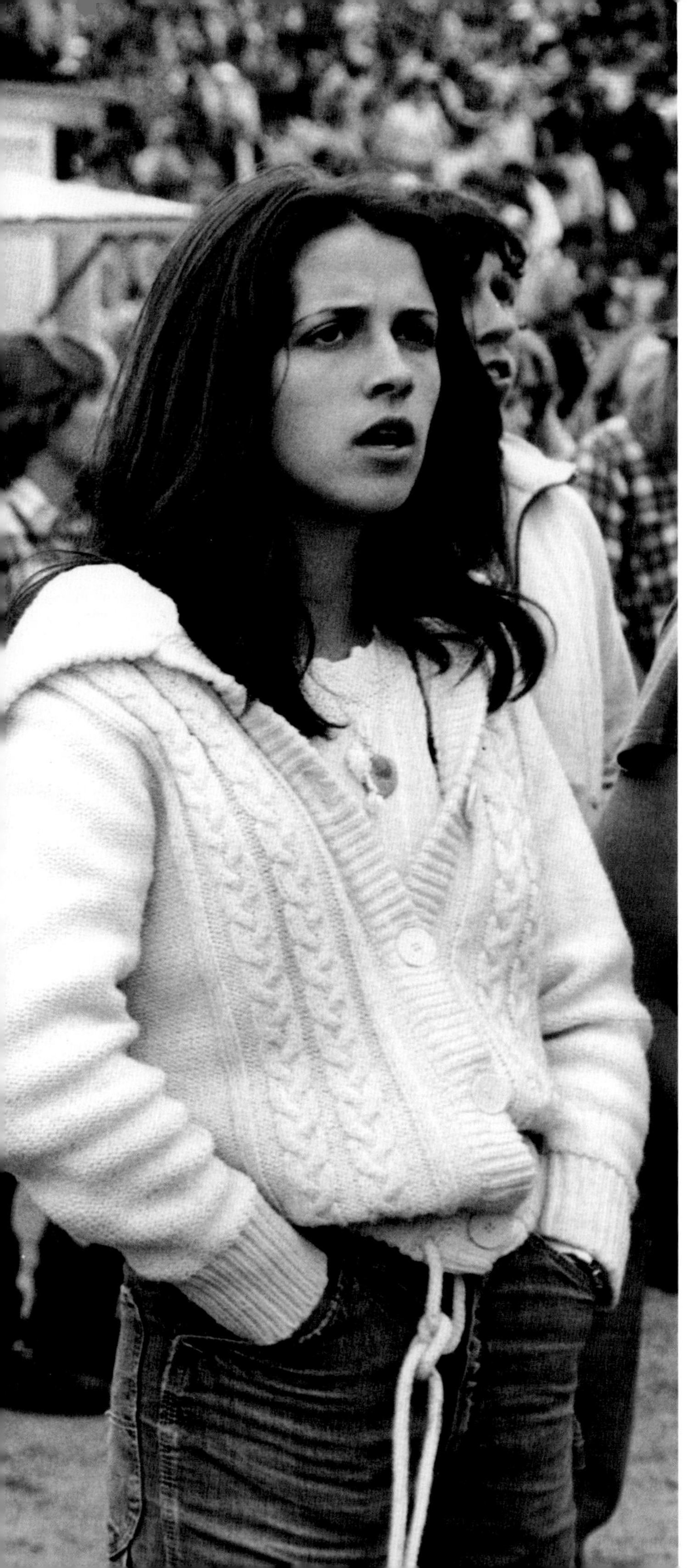

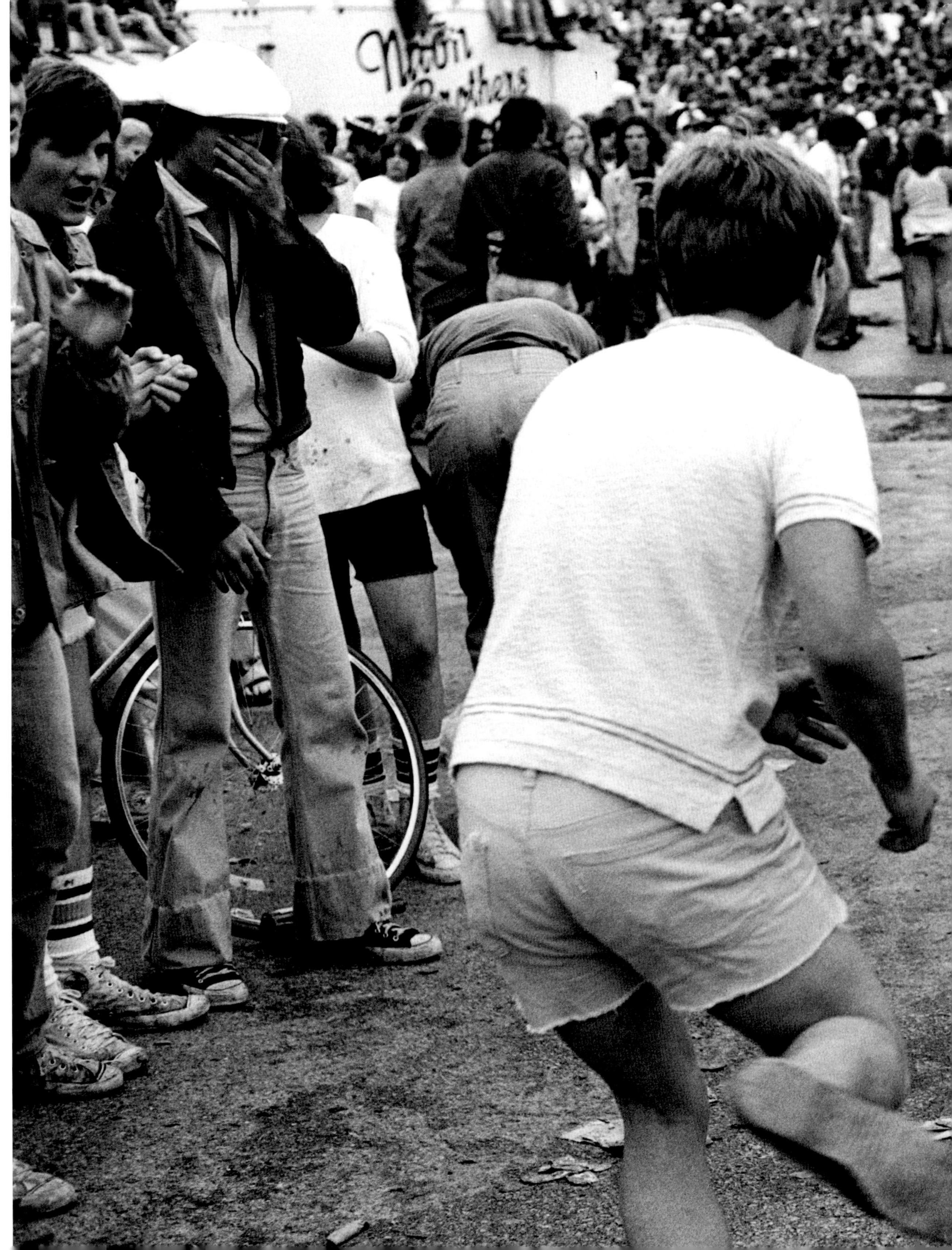

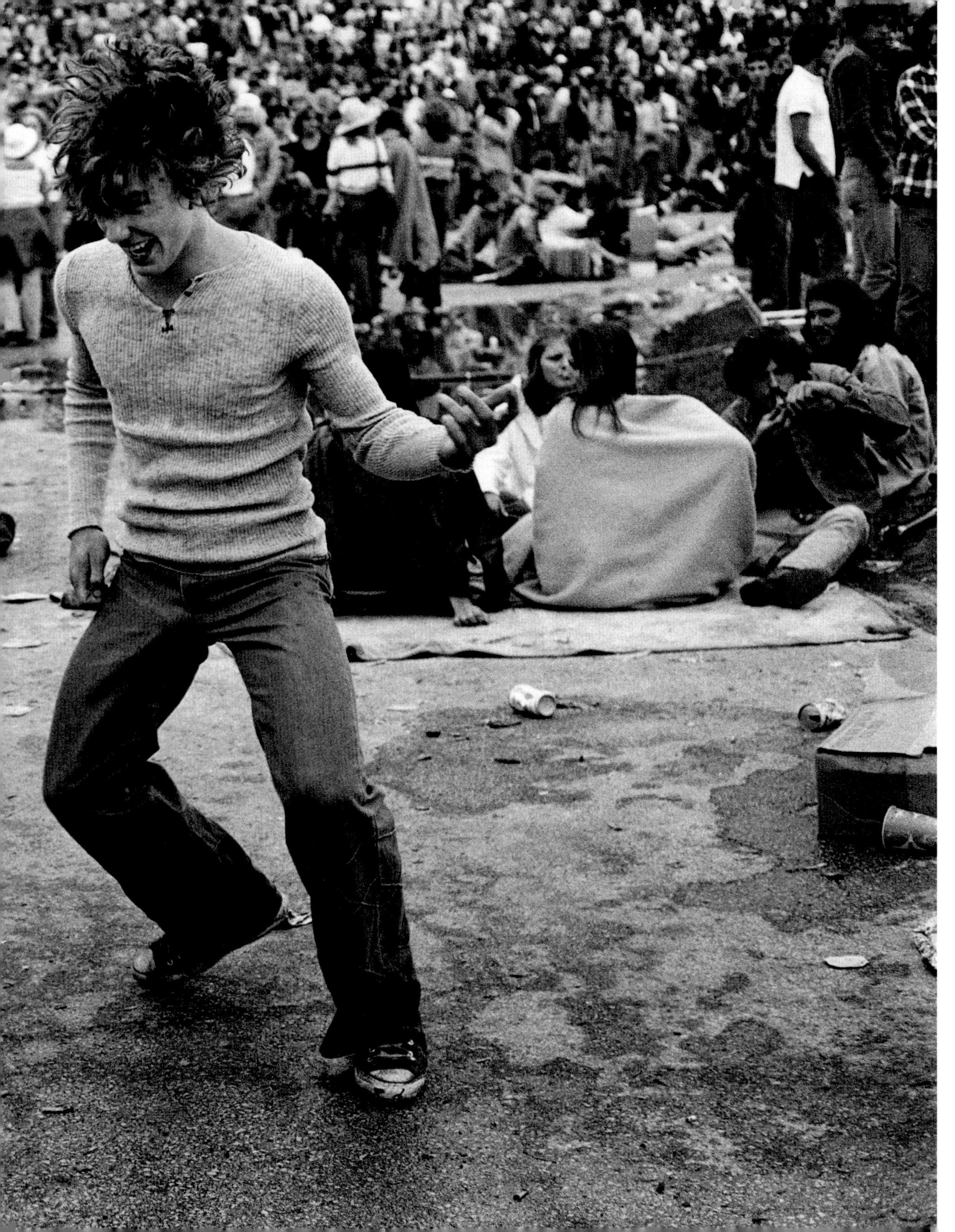

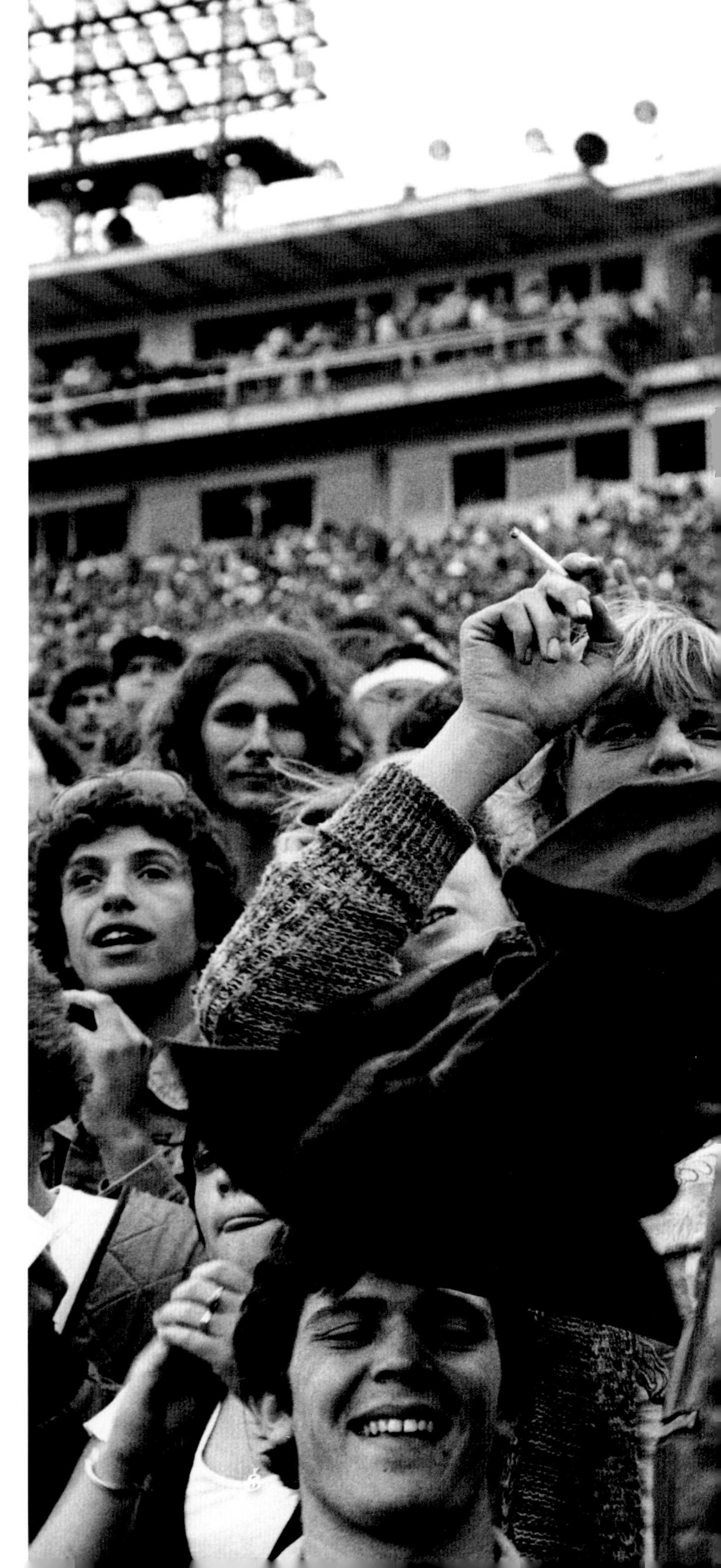

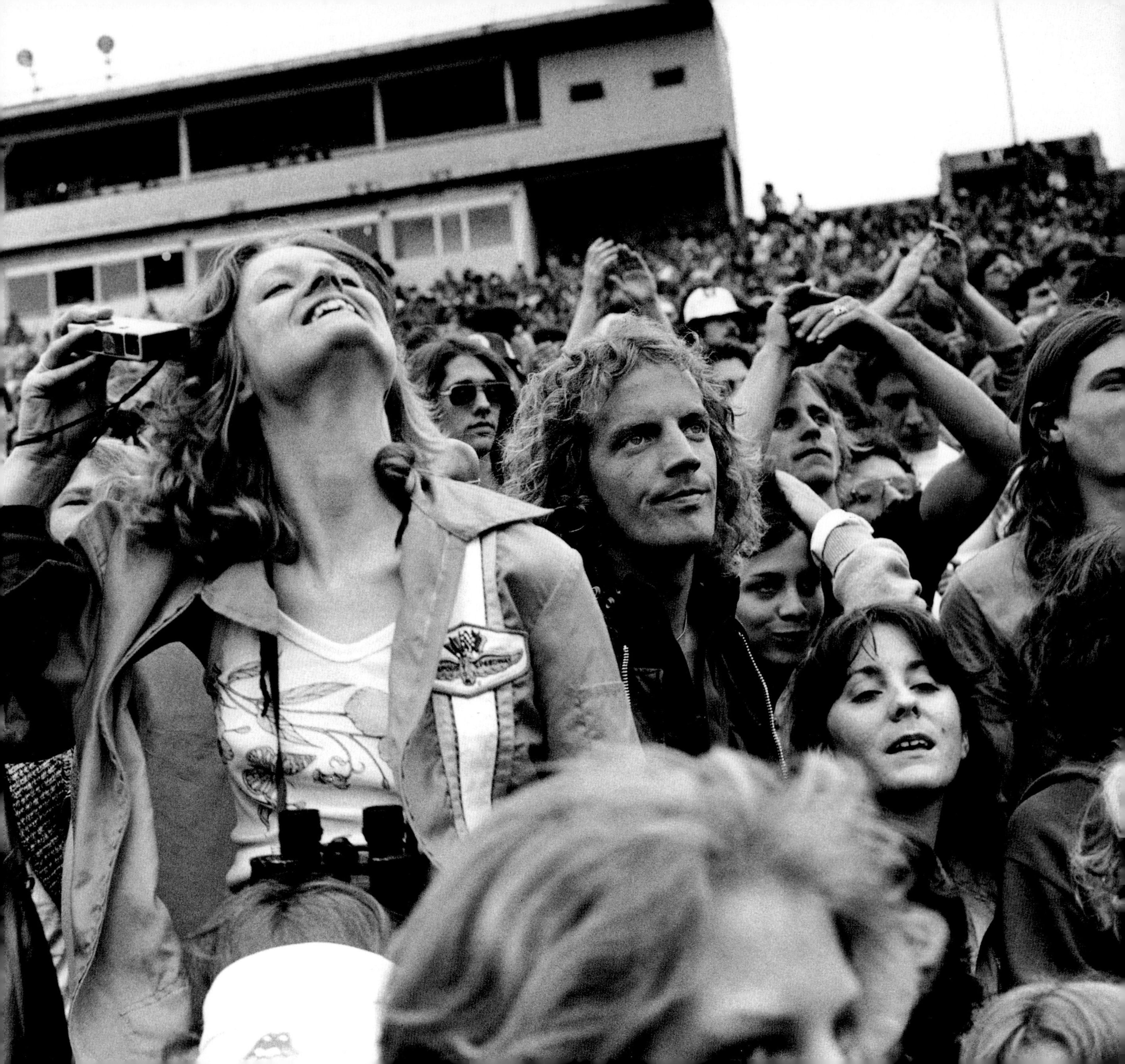

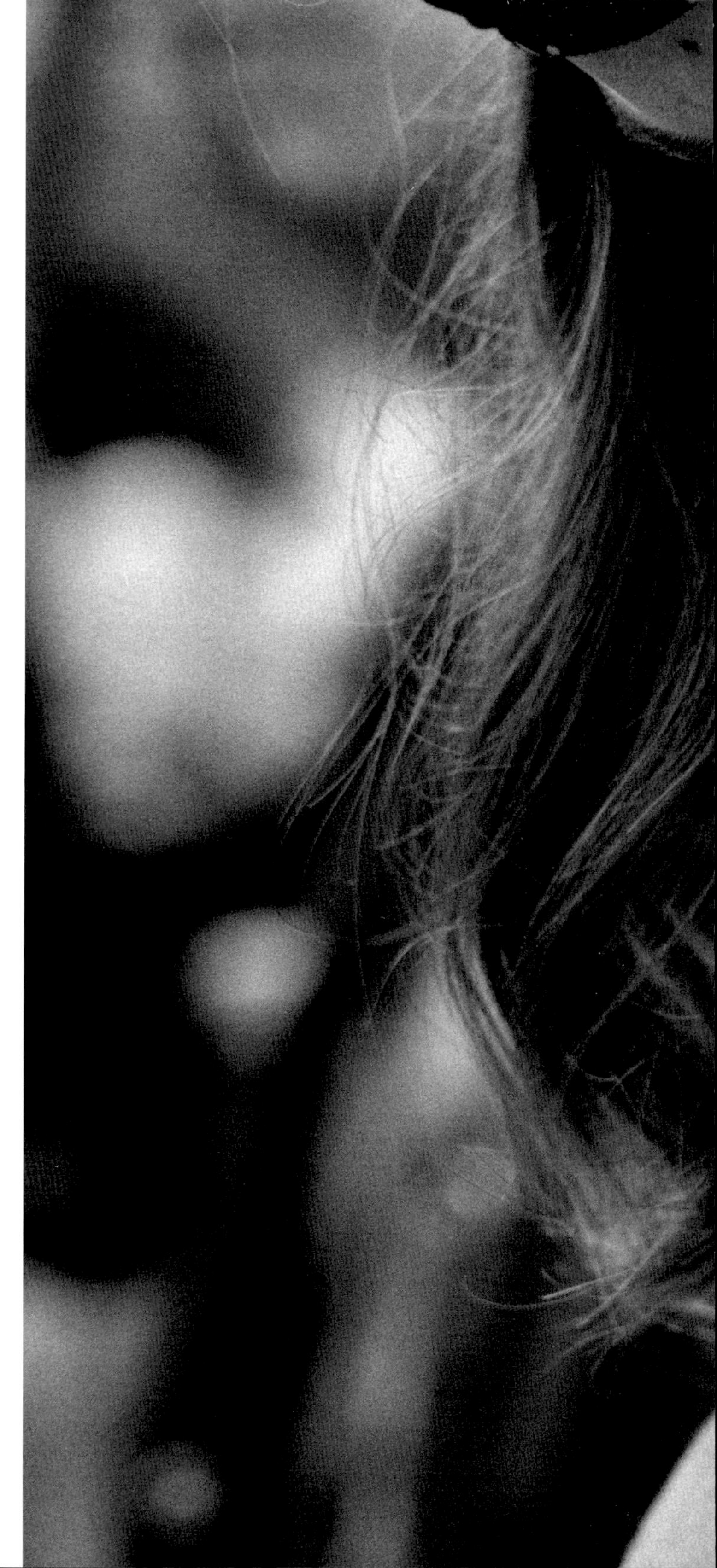

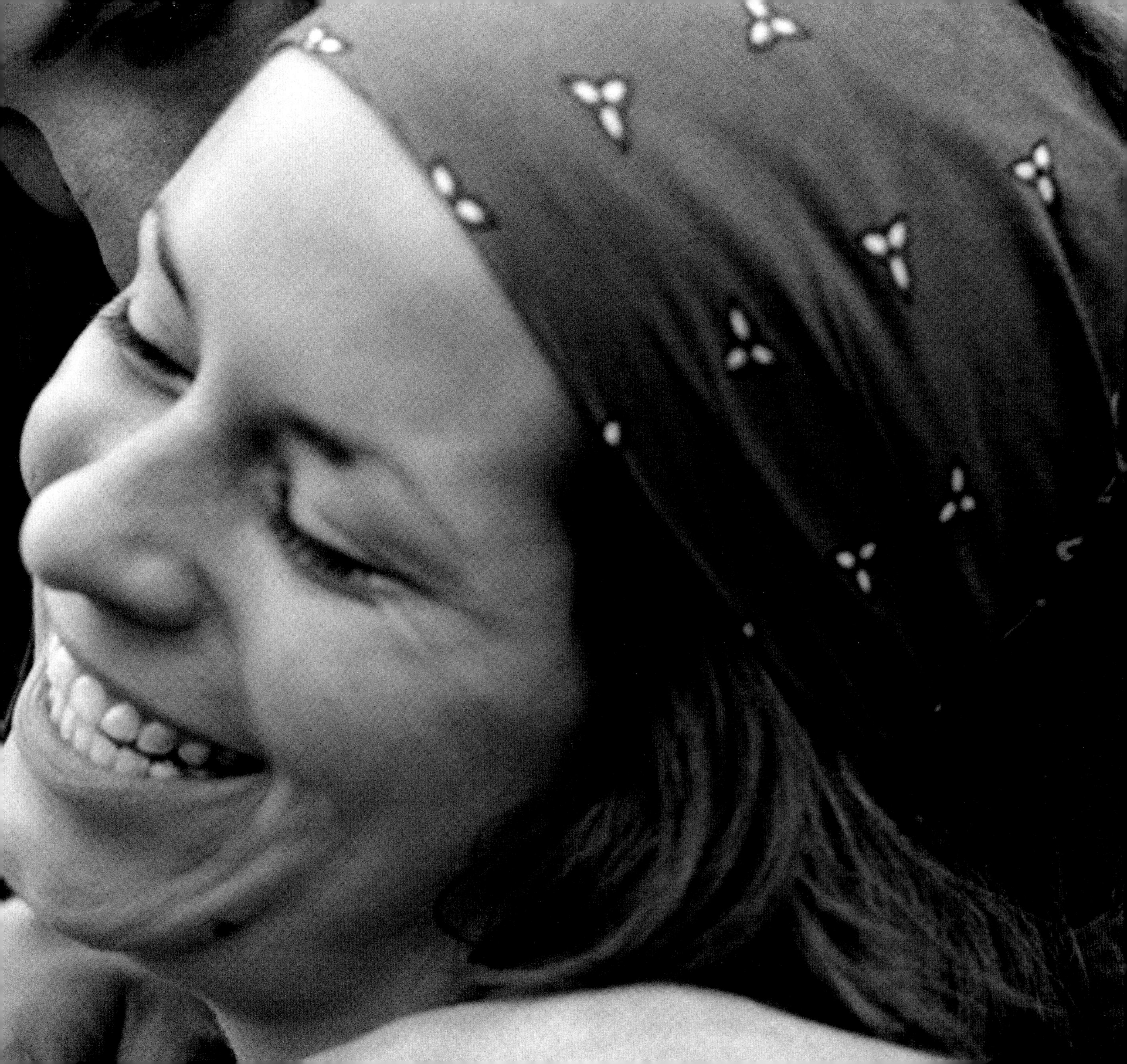

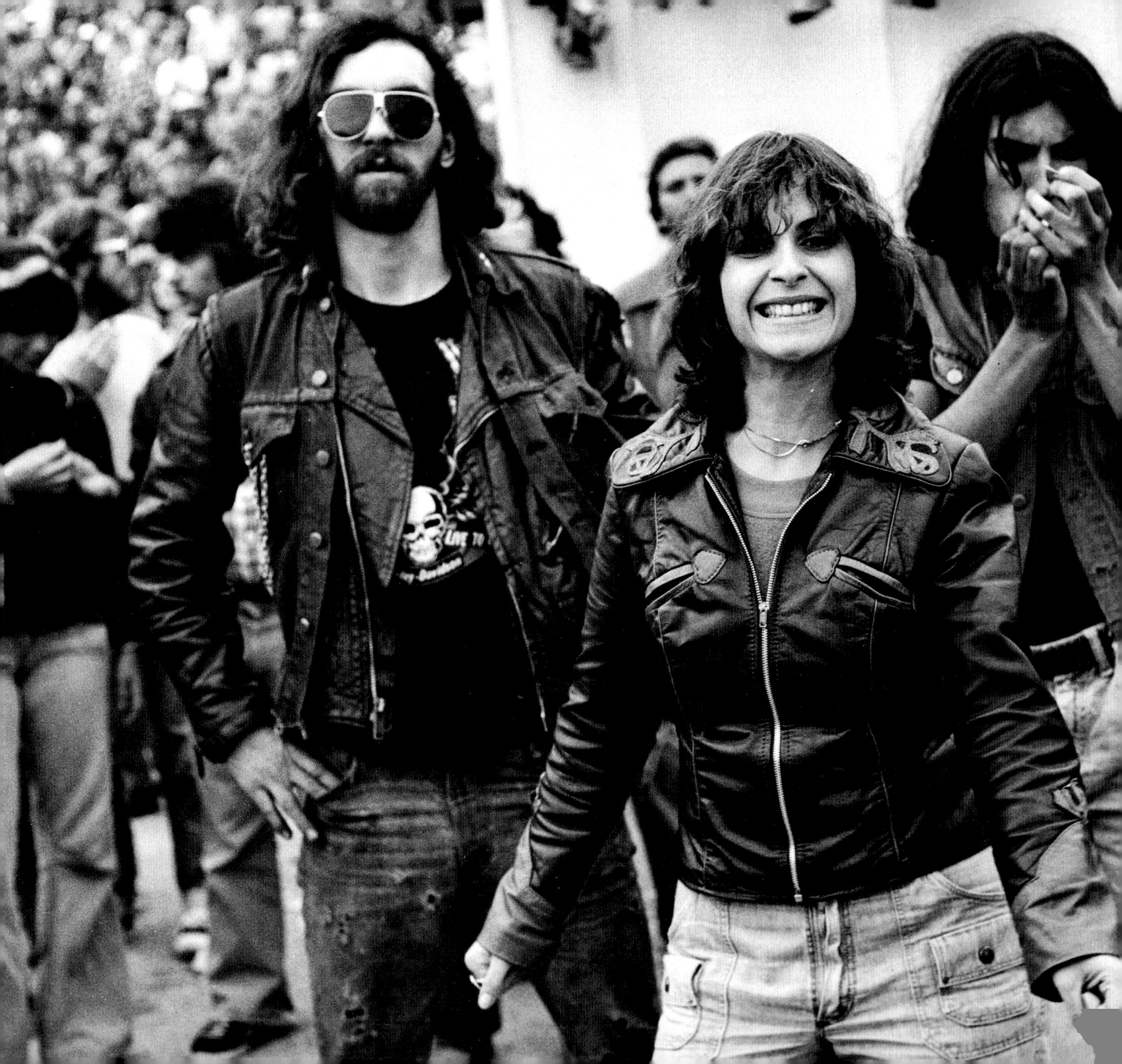

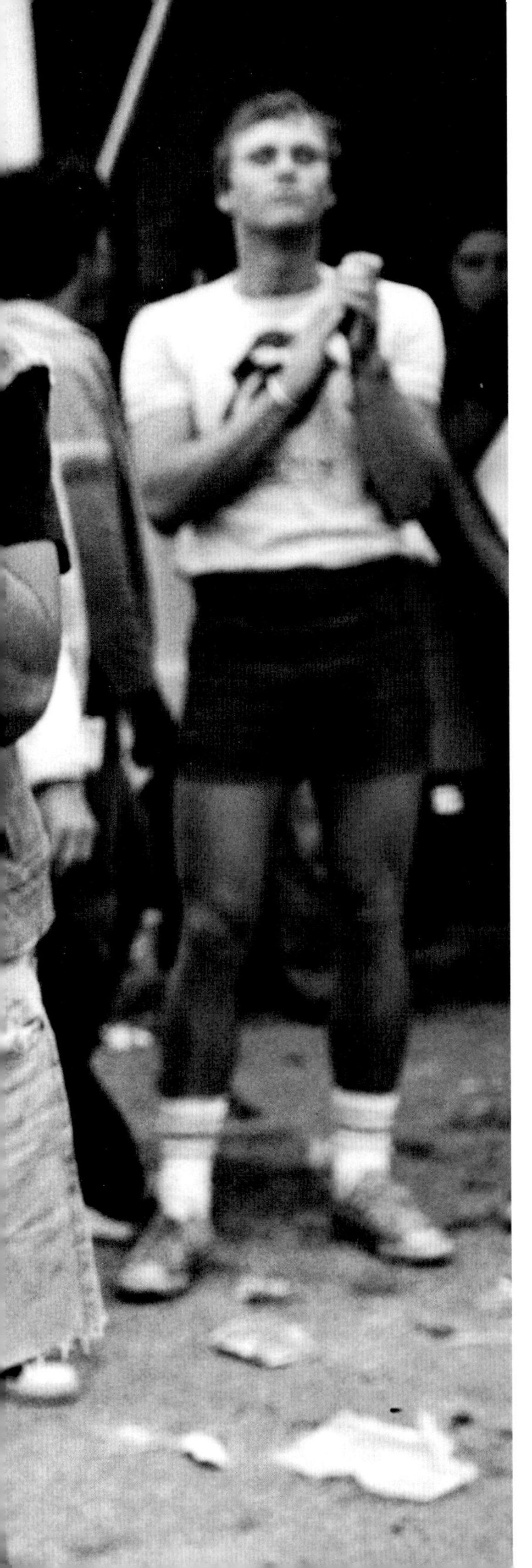

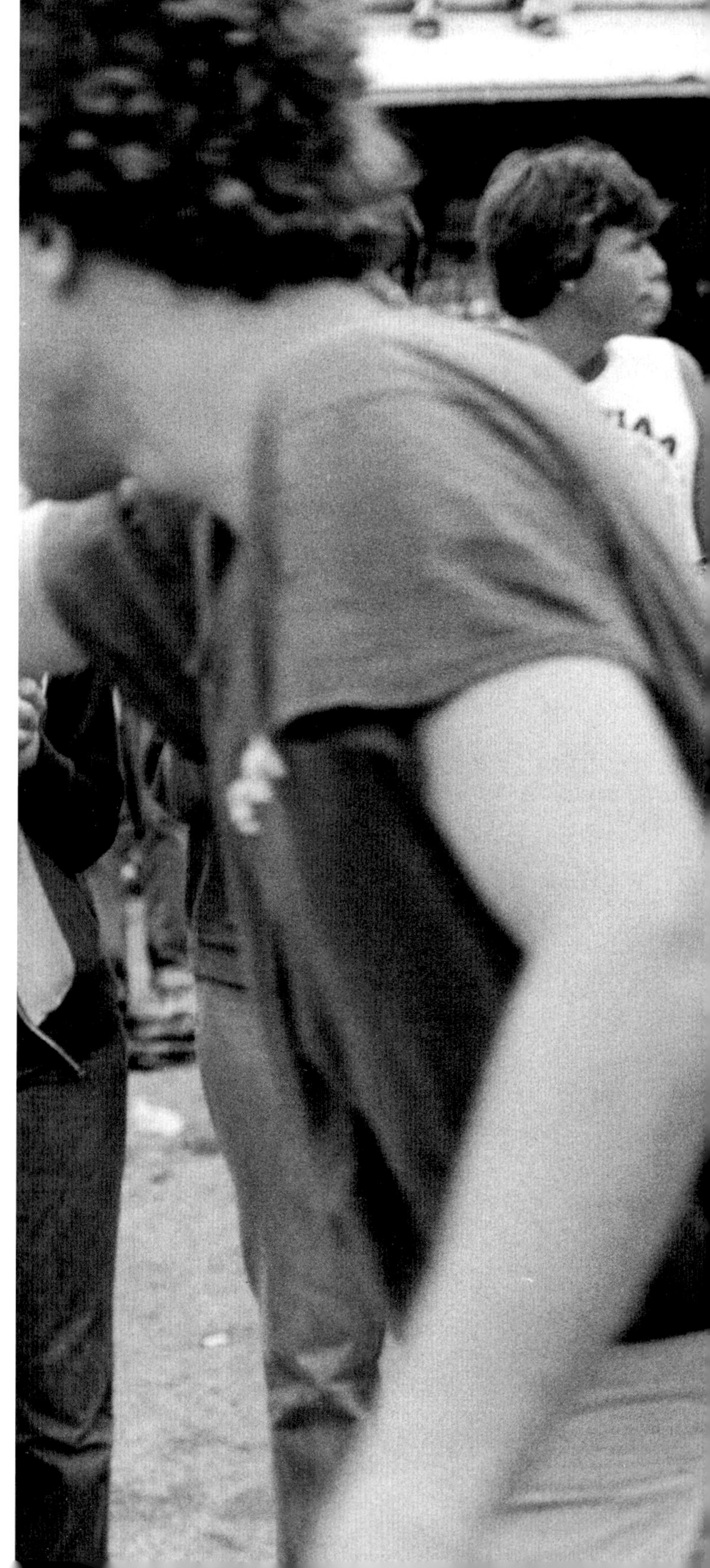

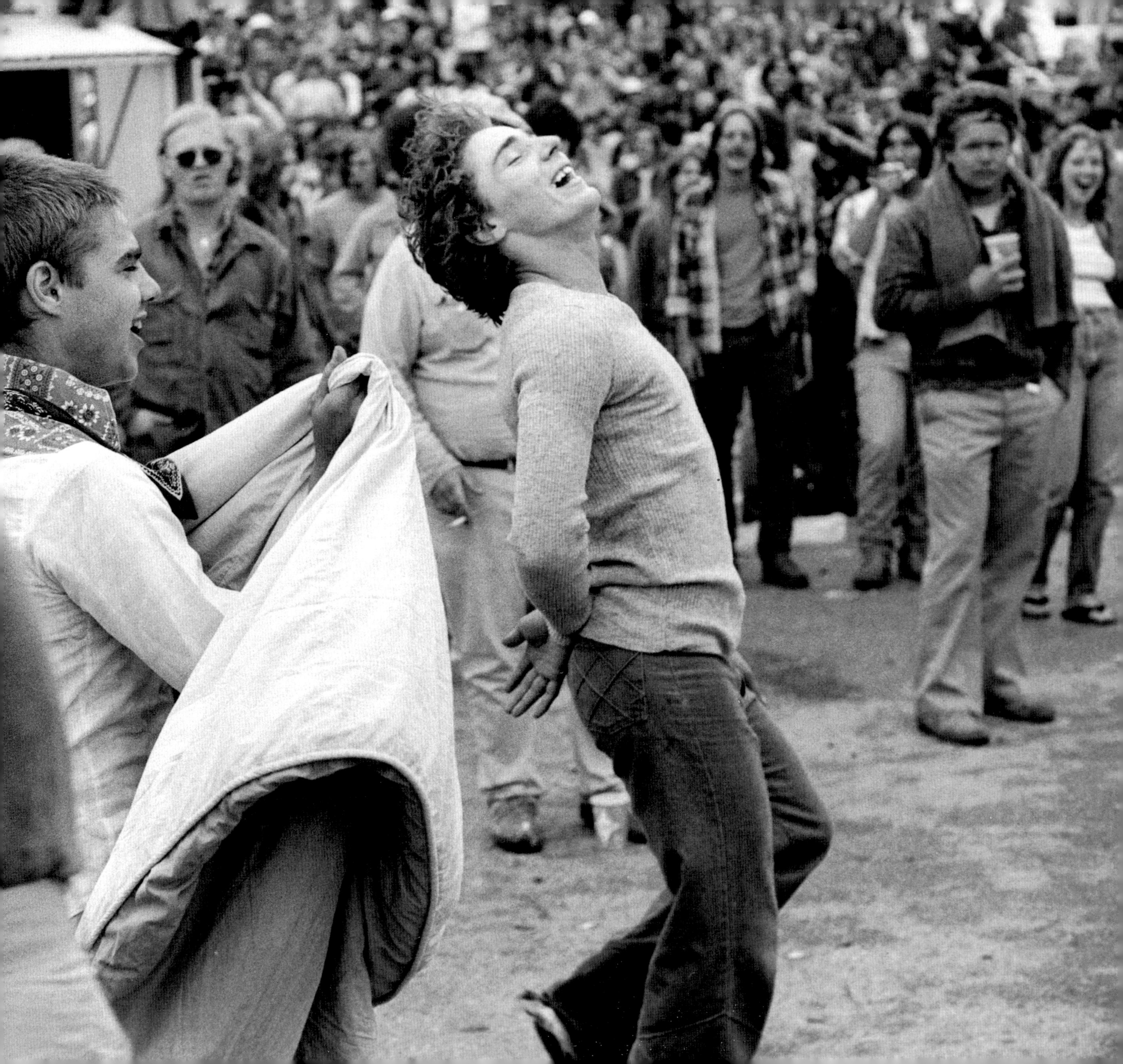

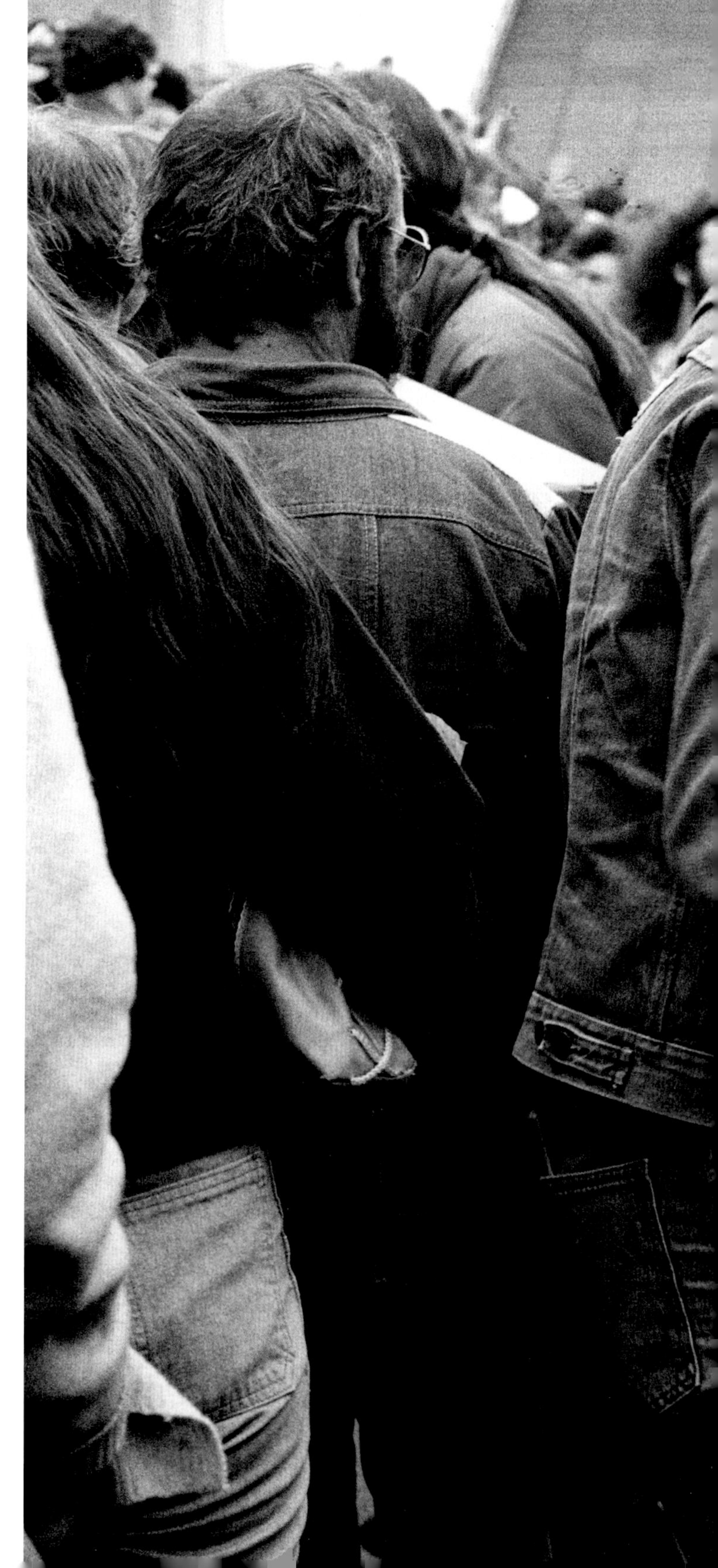

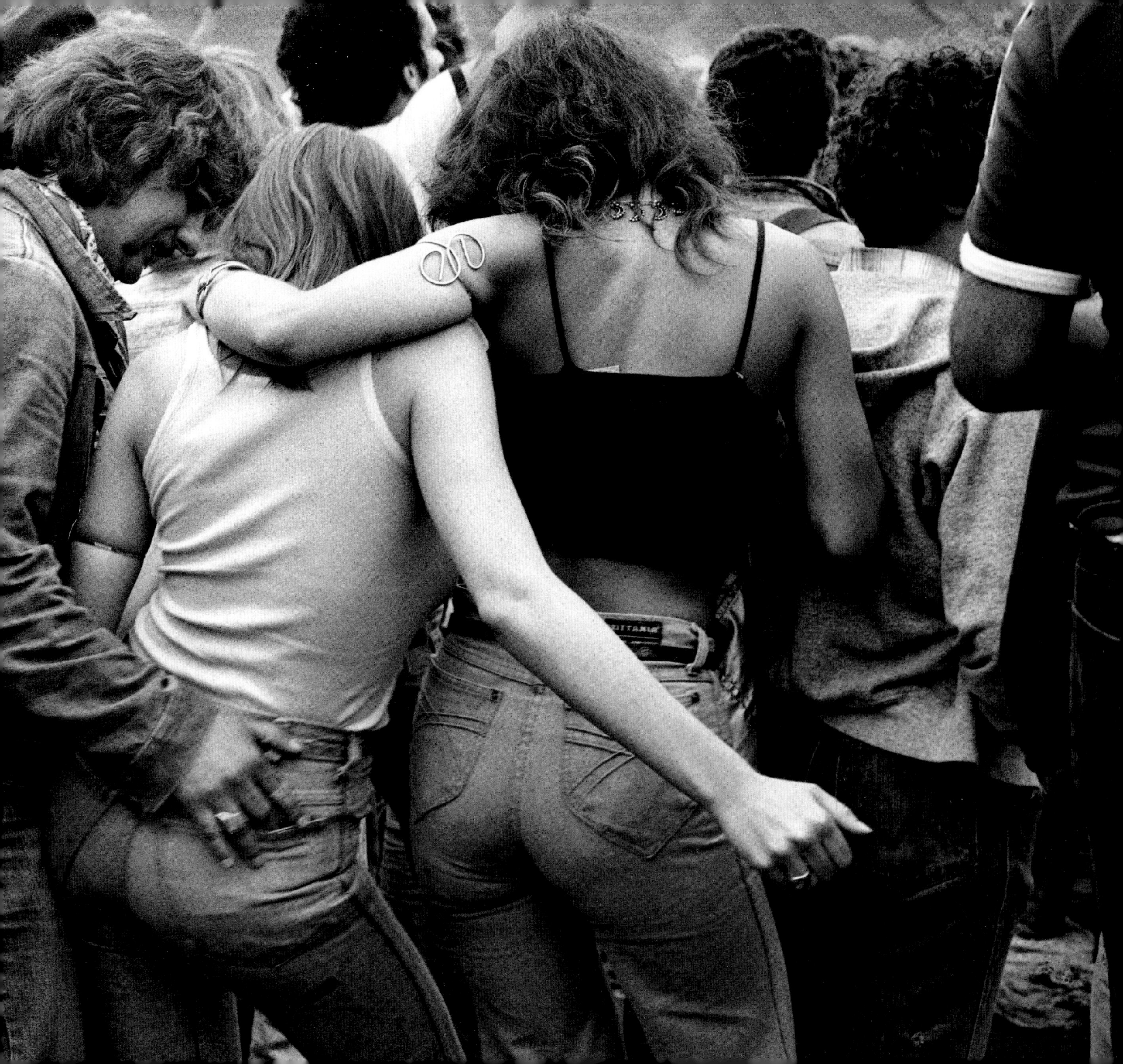

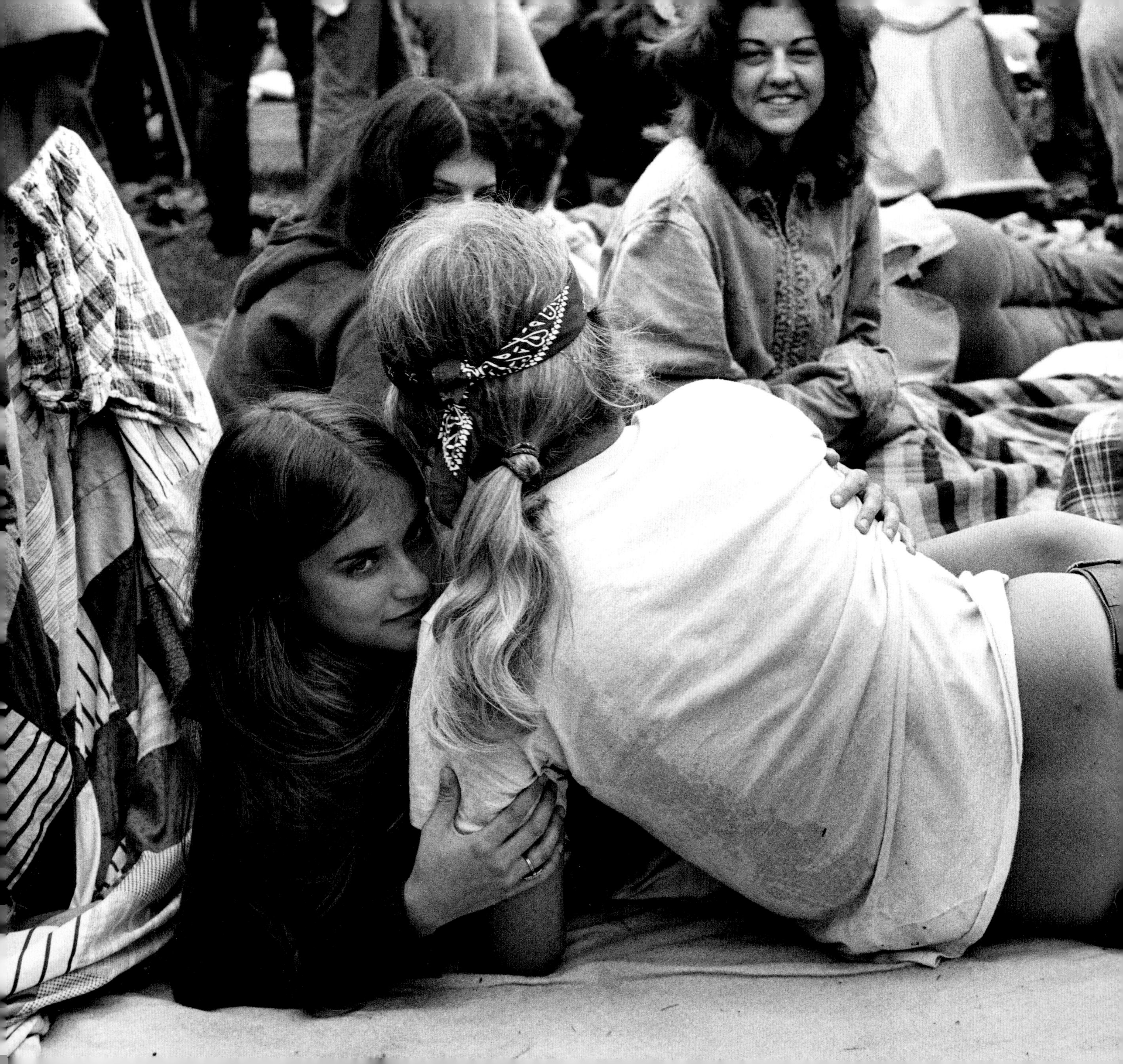

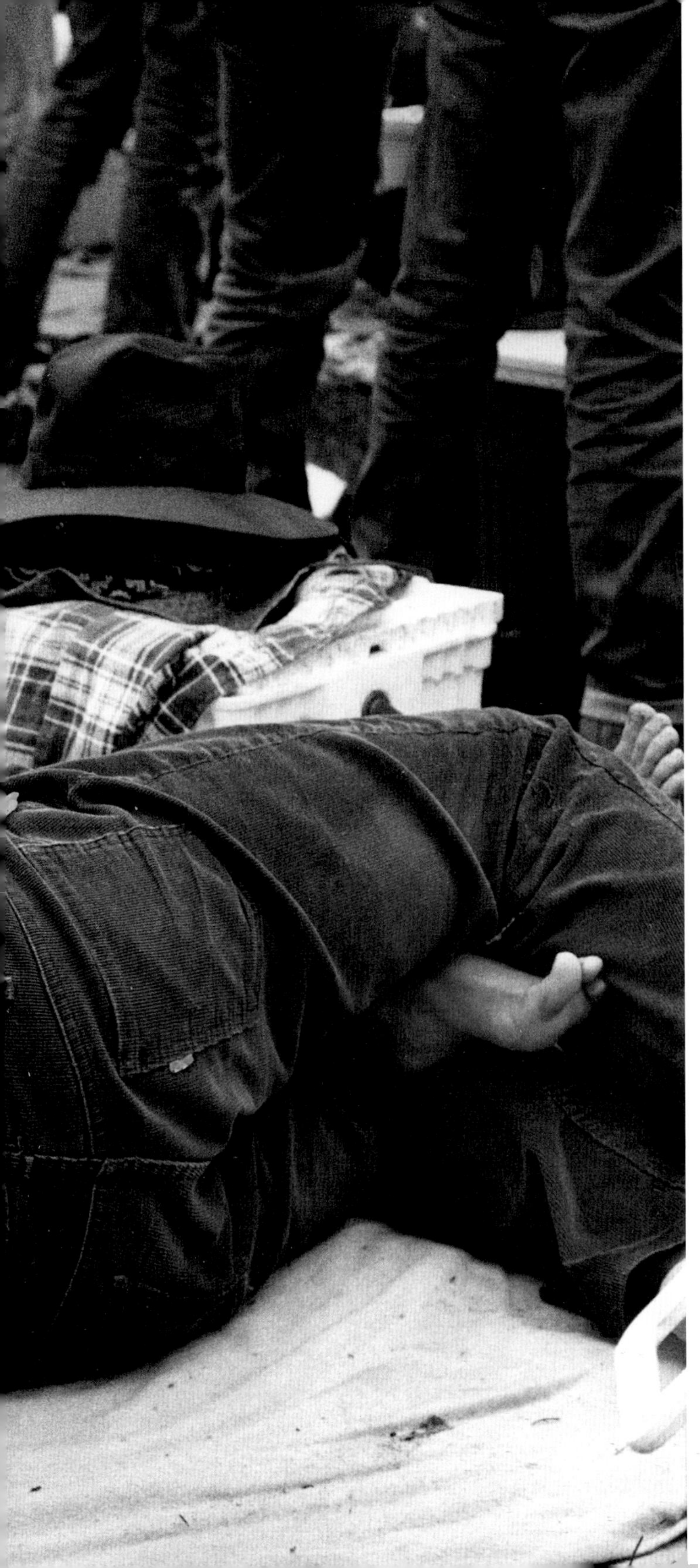

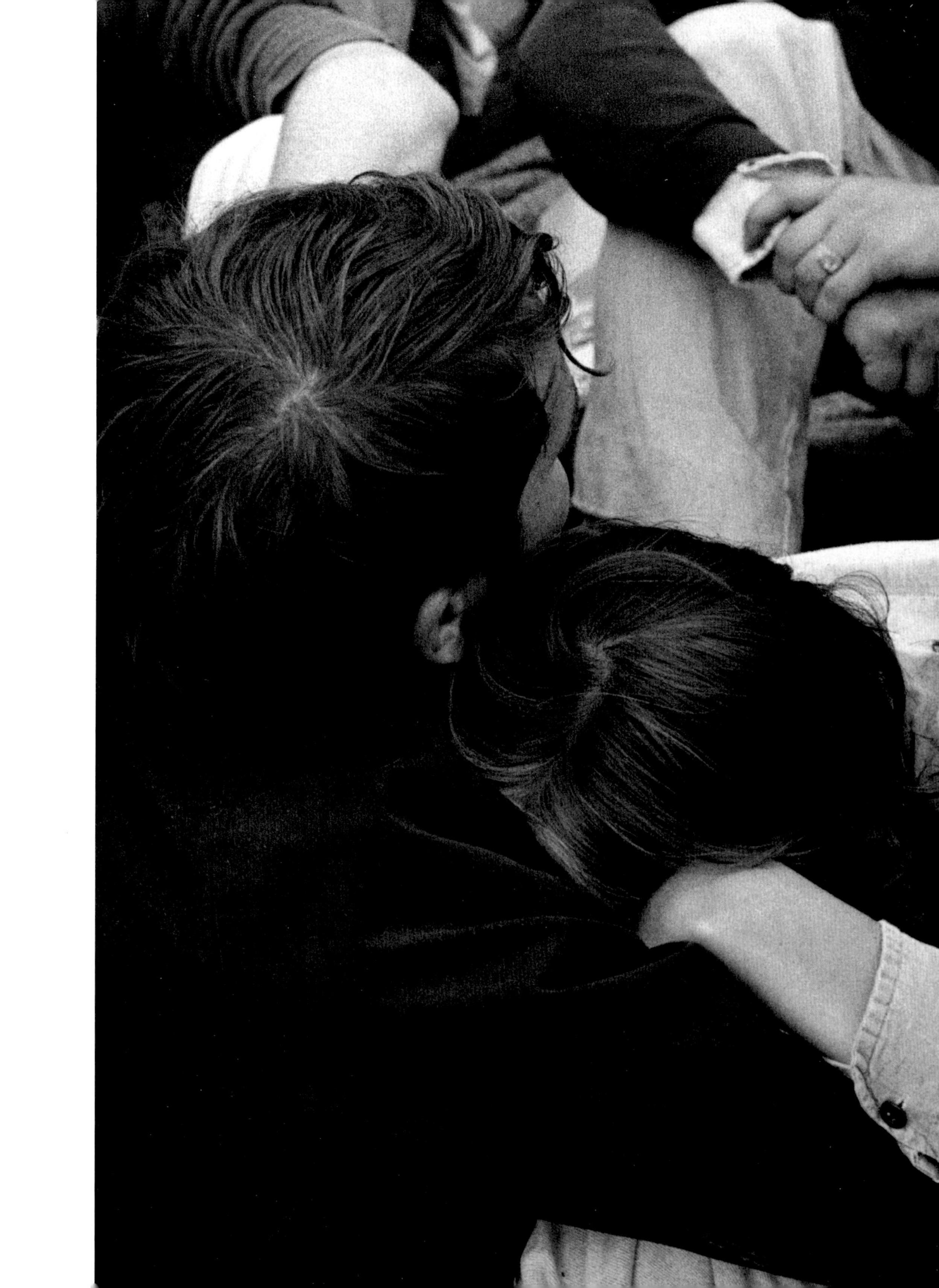

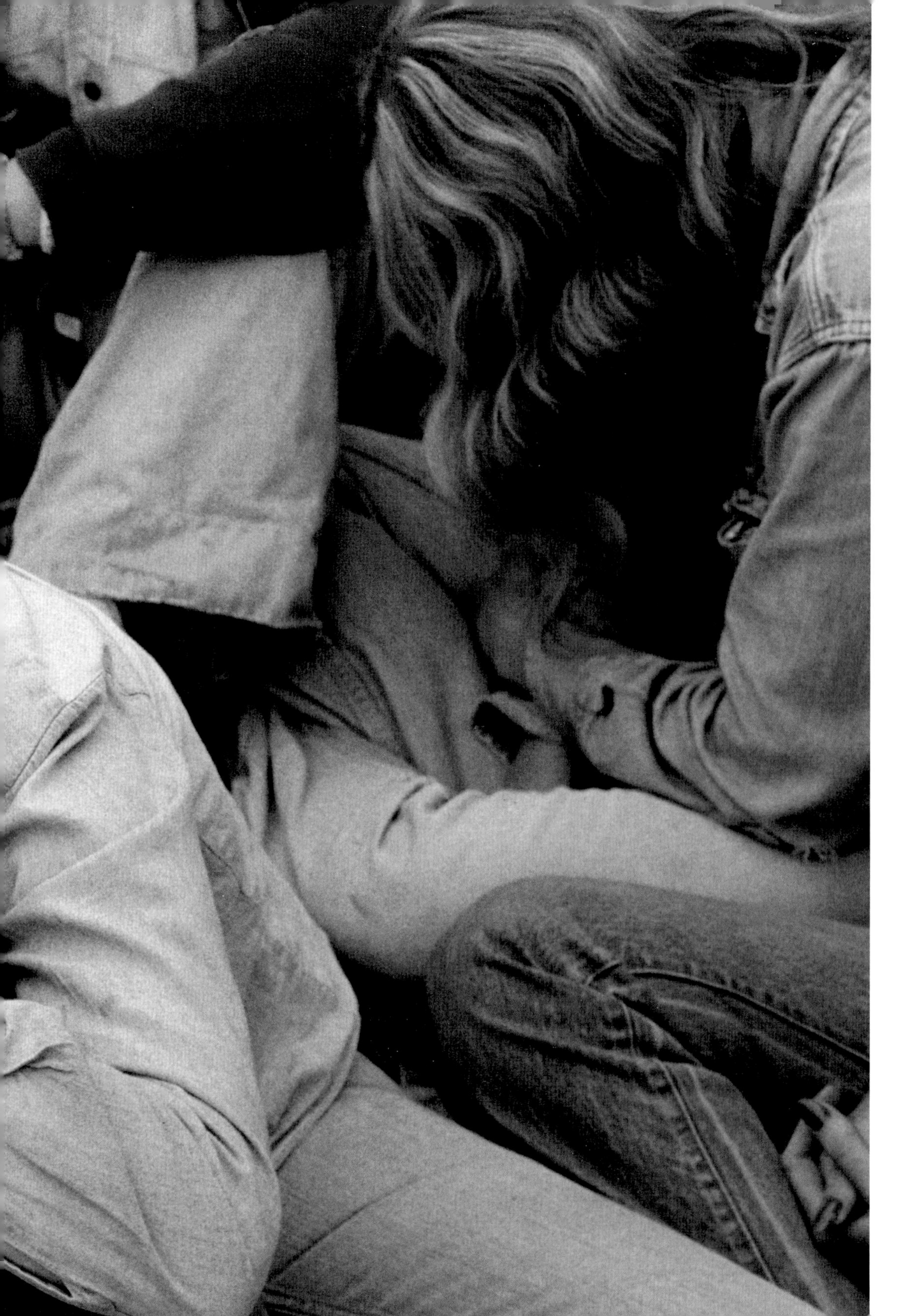

SPECIAL THANKS

I am most grateful to the following family and friends
for all their help and advice in doing the ROLLING STONES FANS book.

Phil Bicker for his total dedication for editing and book design.
Chris Davies and Bill Carraro who made the trip and photographs possible.
George P. Pozderec and David Khachatorian for their interviews and insights.

My family especially Nancy for her loving support, and for Matt, Stacy and Pete.
My publisher, Alex Galán at DAP and Andrea Albertini at Damiani. Hayden Anderson,
Leslie Simitch, Rachael Pony Cassells, Howard Schafferman, Norman Shapiro, Bruce Weber,
Michael Hoppen, Benjamin Trigano, Shannon Richardson, and Tom Gitterman.

And GRACE CODDINGTON for contributing a forward to my book.

National Endowment for the Arts Visual Arts Fellowship in Photography

Joseph Szabo – Rolling Stones Fans

Book Design by Phil Bicker

DAMIANI

Damiani
Bologna, Italy
info@damianieditore.com
www.damianieditore.com

Printed in January 2015 by Grafiche Damiani, Italy.

ISBN 978-88-6208-399-7

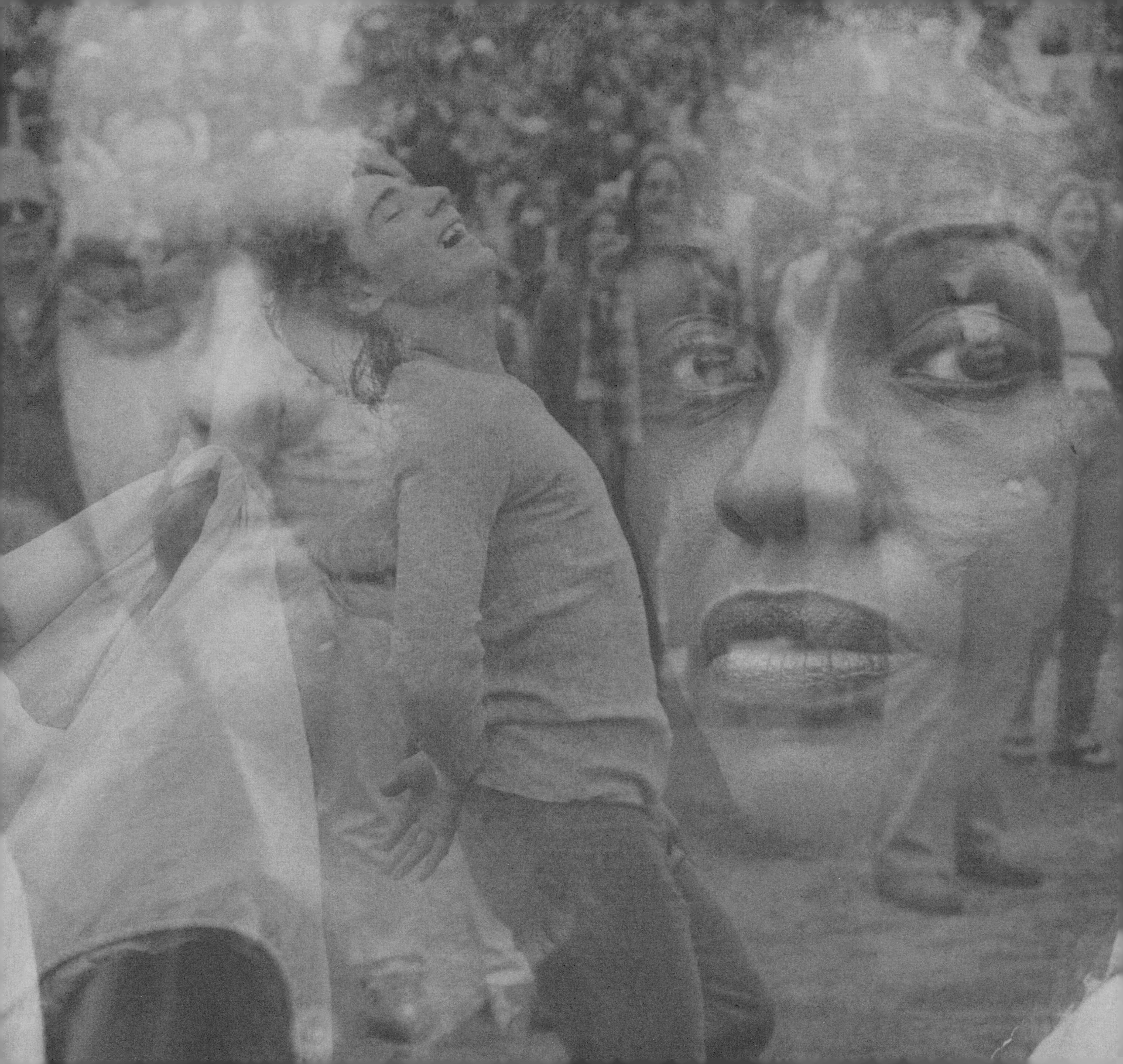

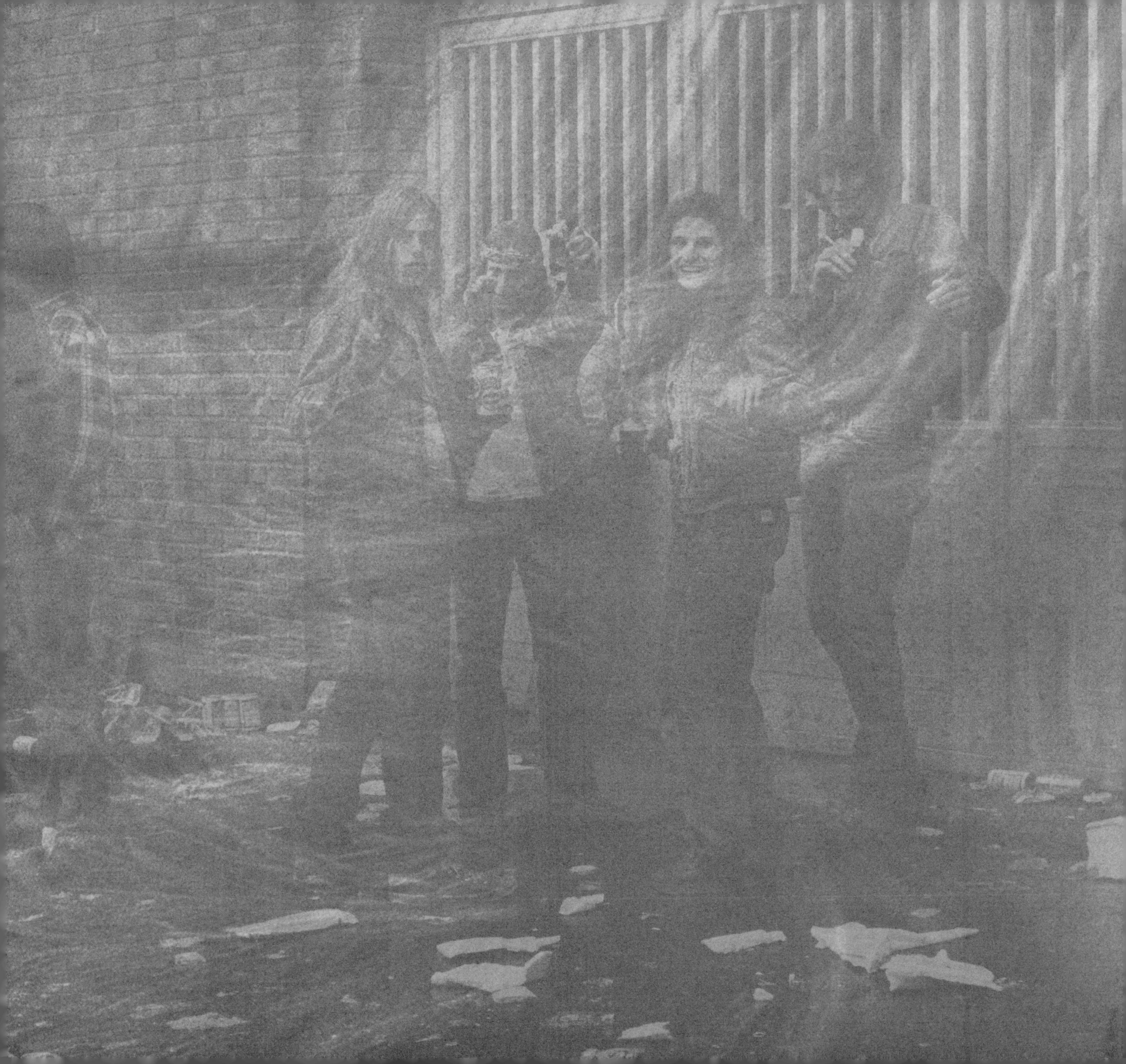